Get Ready for an Amazing Ride

Thankology is like a treasure chest sent to your doorstep by a dear friend. Lisa's inviting, heartwarming and awe-inspiring writing shows us how thank-yous can be felt. Please, open your heart and get ready for an amazing ride.

— **Jen Shang,** Author of *Meaningful Philanthropy*, and Co-Founder and Co-Director, Institute for Sustainable Philanthropy

An Essential Guide

With *Thankology*, Lisa Sargent is nearly asking you to mark the book up. The examples, the visuals, the built-in checklists throughout, it just makes everything so actionable. An essential guide for anyone who wants to be good at making good in the world.

— **Tim Sarrantonio,** Director of Corporate Brand Marketing, Neon One

A Toolkit for Lasting Connections

What truly sets *Thankology* apart from other fundraising resources is Sargent's willingness to freely and open-heartedly share her experiences. She provides real-world examples and best practices that she has perfected over years of hands-on work. The most valuable aspect of *Thankology* is its practical advice – rich with examples and clear strategies – that fundraisers can immediately implement to see tangible results. It's more than just a guide; it's a toolkit for building lasting connections with donors through the power of a simple, heartfelt thank you.

Whether you're new to the field or a seasoned professional, *Thankology* delivers value at every level. New fundraisers will benefit from its clear, step-by-step guidance on cultivating donor relationships, while seasoned professionals will find advanced strategies to refine and elevate their gratitude practices and messaging.

In today's competitive fundraising landscape, *Thankology* is an indispensable asset. It shifts the focus from merely acquiring donors to cultivating and sustaining meaningful relationships. For any fundraising professional dedicated to fundraising excellence, *Thankology* is a vital resource.

— **Jane Nicholson,** Annual Giving Manager, Natural Resources Foundation of Wisconsin

Pure Gold for Fundraisers

In *Thankology*, Lisa Sargent tells it like it is. Gratitude isn't complicated. It's everything. This book will teach you how a simple thank you can turn the tide, win the day, and make your work unforgettable. No fluff, no filler – just the raw, essential truth about the power of saying thanks. For fundraisers, this book is pure gold.

I'm sending *Thankology* to every CEO of every organization that never sent me a proper thank you. That's a lot of books, and a lot of bad manners. Maybe this will remind them of what they're missing.

— **Roger Craver,** Author of *Retention Fundraising* and Editor, The Agitator

Keep More Donors and Raise More Money

Fundraisers know a lot about asking, but not much about thanking. That's a problem. It's likely part of the reason for our industry's abysmal donor retention. Finally, there's help: *Thankology* is a wise, experienced, practical guide to thanking donors. This amazing (and fun) book will help you thank donors with passion, joy, and respect. You'll keep more donors and raise more money.

— **Jeff Brooks,** Author of *The Fundraiser's Guide to Irresistible Communications and How to Turn Your Words Into Money*, and Future Fundraising Now Blog

The Book All Fundraisers Need to Read

Lisa, wonderful Lisa! By writing *Thankology*, she has done something amazing and I am grateful to her. *Thankology* is the book that all fundraisers need to read, then share with their colleagues throughout their organization. Lisa graciously provides you with samples and examples of phrases and ways that you can thank your donors and that you can use immediately. Ways to thank that I hadn't even thought of! And for those who need it, she gives tangible and measurable proof of the importance of thanking donors to increase both retention and giving. *Thankology* shows us how to thank and celebrate donors for their passion and dedication to making the world a better place. *Thankology* will become a staple of my library. Lisa, thank you for your vision. Thank you for creating this book.

P.S. *Thankology* should be required reading for every fundraiser who has ever received a gift from a donor.

— **Glynis Corkal,** Development Officer, Health Sciences Centre Foundation, Winnipeg, MB

Get Your PhD in Thankology

Read Lisa's book and gain the knowledge and skills needed for a Ph.D. in *Thankology*. Whether new to fundraising or a seasoned veteran, this book will make you stop and evaluate your organization's thank-you process. The abundance of Lisa's ready-to-use tools and tips makes it easy to begin improving donor gratitude right away while simultaneously building and strengthening donor engagement in your organization's mission.

— **Ellen Waltimyer,** Development Manager,
Katonah Village Library, NY

It's All Here In One Book

"Always deliver more gratitude than expected," the mantra goes. That's not just a lovely sentiment, worthy of its own throw pillow. Thoughtful thanking drives extraordinary fundraising success. Lisa Sargent is renowned for her soaring, swooning, sensitive and sincere Thankology. Her new book by the same name shares everything she knows ... and I mean everything!

Never has there been a book like this if your goal is to go from mildly thankful ... to masterfully and memorably thankful. How are your thanks? Learn from the wizard: Lisa Sargent.

— **Tom Ahern,** Best-selling author of seven fundraising books and named
one of America's Top 25 Fundraising Experts

Endless Practical Takeaways

Long before gratitude was in the self-help Zeitgeist, Lisa was a knowledgeable, eloquent, and dedicated champion of that most powerful and human thing in fundraising – and its huge impact on retention and lifetime value. So it's no surprise to find *Thankology* crammed with humanity, wisdom and beauty – and endless practical takeaways for you to make your donors feel like the legends they are. Thank you Lisa (and Designer Sandie).

— **Colin Skehan,** Director of Revolutionise Europe, and
Winner Irish National Fundraiser of the Year 2018

Thank-ology

-ology

How to keep your donors longer, and giving stronger, through gratitude

By Lisa Sargent

FOREWORD BY KEN BURNETT

Title: Thankology: A fundraiser's guide to keeping your donors longer, and giving stronger, through gratitude / Lisa Sargent.

Names: Sargent, Lisa 1963- author.

Identifiers: ISBN 9781998796151 (softcover) | ISBN 9781998796168 (EPUB)

Subjects: LCSH: Fundraising | LCSH: Emotions

Publisher: Civil Sector Press
Box 86, Station C, Toronto, Ontario, M6J 3M7 Canada
Telephone: 416.267.1287

www.charityinfo.ca | www.hilborn-civilsectorpress.com

Editors: Jerry Cianciolo, Marlena McCarthy, and Jim Hilborn

Book design:
Sandra Collette, S. Collette Design

We acknowledge that the land where we live and work is the traditional territory of many nations from across Turtle Island, and is covered by the Dish With One Spoon Wampum Belt Covenant, an agreement between the Haudenosaunee and the Ojibway and allied nations, including the Mississaugas, the Anishnaabeg, the Chippewa, and the Wendat peoples to peaceably share and care for the lands around the Great Lakes of North America. This land today is home to many diverse First Nations, Inuit, and Métis peoples. We honour and thank them for their stewardship of these lands, and stand committed to be partners in truth-seeking, healing, reconciliation, and justice for all.

To Matt – and to Giuseppina – who believed first.
To Sophia, who shines a light all her own.
And to Sandie, who makes all the words more beautiful.

ACKNOWLEDGMENTS

There are maybe three people in the world who know I waited until the very end to write these acknowledgments. Now you know too, because you're that kind of wonderful – thank you. For a book that took a decade (not joking, ten years) to come to fruition, I'm deeply worried I'll forget someone. But here goes...

With all my heart, thank you:

<u>To my family</u>. There are no words. (Which you know means, *"Lisa will now immediately say words."*) You kept the faith, did the dishes, listened to rambles, believed when I didn't, hugged when nothing else worked, and loved no matter what. My Matt & Sophia, Maisey Daisy, the best.

<u>To Sandie Collette</u> a.k.a. Designer Sandie, my work wife :), genius designer, CEO of S. Collette Design, and my best friend, who did the design for *Thankology* and almost every other project I'm involved in, fundraising direct response included. There is no creative magic without you. For superb design, for rescuing me daily, for 20+ years of fundraising smarts (and chickies and duckies).

<u>To Ken Burnett</u>, my fundraising hero and friend, who took a chance on me through SOFII, who wrote this book's foreword, and who refused to allow me to abandon *Thankology*. You cheered, commiserated, cajoled, kept track, and more than once gave me a badly needed kick-in-the-butt when the manuscript stalled.

<u>To the late Jerry Cianciolo</u>, editor of Emerson & Church, who led *Thankology* through five (FIVE) rounds of edits before Civil Sector Press and Jim Hilborn took over. Jerry, somewhere in heaven I hope the coffee is just how you like it. This book is better because of you.

<u>To Jim Hilborn and Mary Singleton</u> of Civil Sector Press, for seeing *Thankology* to the finish line... finally!

<u>To SOFII</u>, the Showcase of Fundraising Innovation and Inspiration, for being home to the thank-you clinics that started it all, and forever world-class.

<u>To my nonprofit client family</u>: someone once said to me, *"don't fall in love with your clients."* I threw that advice out the window and never looked back – I love you all, past and present. <u>With extra special thanks to</u>: Merchants Quay Ireland (MQI), Trócaire, St. Helena Hospital Foundation, ChildVision, Kids In Distress, Best Friends Animal Society, Northwestern Memorial

Foundation, and Paul Seigel (a class all his own).

To the stellar fundraisers, colleagues, leaders, and friends who have been part of those nonprofits named above, and others across the years, your trailblazing spirits, trust, expertise, and giving hearts come to life on these pages: Michael Mountain, Steven Hirano, Glen Newhart, Mark Dhooge, Ruth Allen, Carol Casey, Tony Geoghegan, Paula Byrne, Emma Murphy, Nick Jones, Colin Skehan, Janine Heavey, Aislinn Murphy, Louise Walker, Ali Lynch, Caoimhe de Barra, Gwen Dempsey, Karen Smyth, Kathryn Michael. And to Denisa Casement, Casement Group CEO and MQI's former head of fundraising: Who knew one little teabag, *"Desperately need a copywriter,"* and Nana Murphy would carry us here.

To T. Clay Buck, for gallows humor, gut-checks, generosity geekery, the WLD, wise feedback, fundraising shop talk, and time-zone-defying friendship.

And also to: Jen Shang, Adrian Sargeant, Roger Craver, Tom Ahern, Marc Pitman, Bill Jacobs, Mark Phillips, Bloomerang, Jeff Brooks (who probably doesn't remember he lit the spark for this book in 2014), Penelope Burk, Steven Screen, Simone Joyaux (forever in our hearts), May-baby buddies Pamela Grow and Erica Waasdorp, Mal Warwick, Moceanic champs Christiana Stergiou and Sean Triner, Lynne Wester, Mary Cahalane (rebels with a cause!), Harvey McKinnon, Bernard Ross, Tim Sarrantonio, Simon Scriver, and SOFII's Joanna Culling, whether through your research, your work, your encouragement, your gracious permission to use samples, your thought leadership, support, friendship, and/or a thousand other reasons, a little idea about the power of gratitude became reality.

To donors. To beneficiaries. To you.

"Remember:
We are not machine-minders but makers
of a better world. Never forget the
distinction between the two."

— George Smith (RIP),
Fundraising legend and author of *Asking Properly*

v

Thank -ology

What's inside

Welcome to the art and science of positive thanking

Foreword, by Ken Burnett

Whoopee! Saying thank you has just got an ology. We should be so, so proud!

An ology is a really big thing in the UK and, well…everywhere. A few years back, in a campaign called 'It's you we answer to', Britain's telecommunications giant BT ran a popular series of television advertisements featuring a lovable but domineering grandmother called Beattie (BT, geddit?), using her telephone to keep in touch with her extended family. In one of these commercials, she rings her grandson Anthony, on a rather special day. The conversation went like this:

> *Beattie:* Anthony? Oh, Anthony. Congratulations on your exam results!
> *Anthony (despondent)*: Grandma, …I failed.
> *Beattie: (shocked)*: What d'you mean, you failed?
> *Anthony* I mean I failed. English, math, physics, geography, German, woodwork, art… I failed!
> *Beattie:* You failed… everything? You didn't get…anything?
> *Anthony* I passed pottery.
> *Beattie:* Pottery? Pottery! Very useful, pottery is. People always need plates Anthony (silent pause). Er…, anything else?
> *Anthony* Sociology.
> *Beattie:* An ology! (pause– sharp intake of breath) He gets an ology, and he says he's failed! Anthony, you got an ology! You get an ology, you're a scientist!
> *Anthony* Oh! Thanks Grandma!
> Voice over explains the reassuring power of a phone call.
> *Beattie:* Oh yes, it's the teachers that are all wrong. You know, they can't mark! A lot of them can't see…

It went viral, before viral was even a thing.

So yes, now, thanks to Lisa Sargent, we campaigning fundraisers have… an ology. Wow! That is so, so special.

Why? What's so special about *Thankology*?

Simple. Saying thank you properly <u>is the best fundraising opportunity of them all</u>, bar none.

It's time we realized this. Time we elevated the subject, right up to where it belongs.

We need to consider it an ology. We need to respect it, study it, excel at it, to value it properly. This book does all that, and more.

You don't believe me? Well, now you can find within these pages shedloads of vibrant, recent, highly copyable examples of the multiple benefits that thankology can bring.

When I started in fundraising (embarrassingly long ago, I confess), thanking donors was considered an expensive and tedious chore. I vividly remember struggling to persuade charities in the UK to even consider saying thank you nicely, to even say thank you at all. Thanking donors then was considered an inconvenient and costly burden that could quite easily be dispensed with. How short-sighted they were!

Of course not thanking someone who's just given you a generous gift is downright rude. I mean, *duh!* Surely our mothers taught us that much? Not thanking a donor because their gift doesn't match your concept of acceptable generosity is also downright rude. Not doing it quickly and effectively is… well, as well as rude it's also stunningly myopic and plain downright foolish. Because in fundraising, saying thank you properly is a sure-fire route to riches.

Anyone who imagines that such a mundane, even dull and routine activity as saying thank you isn't seriously effective and essential work needs their bumps feeling, and no mistake. Yet for sure, puffed-up, self-important organizations by the score will take just such a stance. More the fools, them.

The real absurdity for fundraising outfits that don't thank their donors properly and creatively is that they are so cutting off their own noses to spite their shiny little faces. Because, now we know, thanking properly pays. Big time!

Now through this book *Thankology*, Lisa Sargent shows us that even confirmed evangelists and enthusiasts for thanking have been massively underestimating the income and relationship-building potential of the natural, universal, so human act of saying a simple thank you. Or, in myriad variations, 'welcome, well done, congratulations, you've made a difference, you are great'.

In my early years as a donor-focused fundraiser I feasted gloriously on the great 'bibles' of direct mail – the books and articles of Mal Warwick, Jerry Huntsinger, Denny Hatch and others. Real treasure troves, of course. But in all these I found very, very little that was useful on thank-you letters or on the skills and processes necessary for effective, creative thanking.

Now there is. Now, in this book, it's all there in abundance.

- There wasn't a library of copyable examples of delightful thank-you letters. Now there is.

- There certainly wasn't any explanation of the benefits of thanking, or the techniques of testing how to thank properly. Now there is.

- Nor were there any revelations and insights on effective thanking over the phone. Now there is.

- Back then there was of course no analysis of digital thanking, or saying thanks via social media, or online, or by email. Now there is.

- For sure, no way then was there anything useful about using the insights of thankology successfully for in-memoriam givers, or for annual reports, or even in supporter newsletters. Now there is.

In fact, the subject Lisa so wisely terms 'Thankology' has been explored, explained, expanded and exposed here like never before. In this book you're now holding, there's all that and lots more besides.

- There's how to explain and inspire others in your organization so they'll be as enthusiastic about thankology as you are.

- There's how to reliably and consistently write the best ever heart-lifting, life-affirming and rewarding thank-you letters of all time.

- There's how thankology can underpin and help you to build the very best donor/cause relationships – reliably.

- There's how thankology is crucial, and priceless, if you wish to design and deliver the very best and most durable supporter experiences.

Chapter by chapter the author defines and describes the key milestones of what will be fundraising's latest and perhaps, most lucrative science. *Thankology* doesn't just teach you, it gives you real, concrete, copyable examples on almost every page. Plus, for good measure the author throws in lots of free extra bonuses too.

It's a special privilege for me to write this foreword because the science, art and craft of thankology has its roots in the Lisa Sargent Thank-you Clinics on SOFII.org, that we jointly initiated a dozen or so years ago. To this day they are the most visited exhibits in the entire SOFII archives, bar none (SOFII is the Showcase of Fundraising Innovation and Inspiration, available free 24/7 on www.sofii.org). But in truth I'm also extra-honored because I can see this so accessible, easy to use tome, *Thankology: a fundraiser's guide to keeping your donors longer, and giving stronger, through gratitude* could be the most significant, most immediately beneficial book for campaigning fundraisers in ages. Why? Well, we've known for decades that the favorite subject of people everywhere is, almost invariably, themselves. Almost anything that's about them, that's what, wherever they are, people find most appealing and most listenable-to. If it's about themselves it is everyone's most-loved topic of conversation, what they most love to hear and read about. Themselves. In this book, through the practice of thankology Lisa Sargent has mined this most human of human responses to set out how you, in your supporter communications, can access and apply what Lisa calls 'the intoxicating brain-chemical bath of serotonin, dopamine, and oxytocin that science has proven you can spark with gratitude.' Imagine that! Your attitude of gratitude can ignite all the very ingredients that you want to flood your donors' brains, to make them feel terrific, special, appreciated, warm and generous towards your cause. Get your thankology right, and how powerful will that be?

When BT's Beattie, her voice hushed with wonder and respect, said to her grandson Anthony, 'You've got an ology,' she wasn't exaggerating or soft-soaping him, she was telling him to find and focus on the positives. My mother used to say to me, 'Kenneth, positive things happen to positive thinkers'. I've never forgotten it. Beattie would have approved.

Now we can say, positive things happen to positive thankers. Because, well, we've got an ology. *Thankology*. By Lisa Sargent. We should be eternally grateful.

Ken Burnett,
Suffolk, England
June 2024

PART I:

How to write thank-you letters, emails, and other bite-sized bits of gratitude your donors will love

"What we've got here is failure to communicate."

— Cool Hand Luke

thank you

This book is about helping you do a better job of thanking your donors, and the amazing things that result...

But this book's genesis began years ago, in April 2007.

That's when I read an article that delivered the nonprofit sector's equivalent of the shot heard round the world.

Or at least that's how I interpreted it.

The author was no less than one of the world's foremost experts on philanthropic psychology, Professor Adrian Sargeant (no relation; note additional 'a' in surname). In *The Chronicle of Philanthropy*, he wrote:

Retention is the single biggest issue we face as a sector today.

Then he laid down data that <u>should</u> have stopped every working nonprofit professional in their tracks:

An increase of just 10 percent in donor retention, Sargeant wrote, can yield up to a 200% increase in the lifetime value of your donors.

Two hundred percent!

All you had to do for those seismic results was to keep just one extra donor in ten.

It was a BIG DEAL then. It's a BIG DEAL now.

So big that Adrian Sargeant's words would one day help place this book in your hands.

You see, back in 2007 I already knew donor retention was intimately connected to fundraising returns. And I knew that quality, donor-focused thanking was intimately connected to donor retention.

I knew because I'd just emerged from a handful of years with a single client, helping craft the direct mail and digital donor communications – *communications that radiated gratitude for givers* – of one of the top US animal welfare charities.

At the time their annual revenue was roughly $20 million.

As I write this, they've crested $102 million... a 500+ percent improvement.

I knew without a doubt how thanking donors worked a special kind of magic on retention and revenues.

It is this world-changing magic I want to give to you today.

Now turn the page, and let's give your donors something beautiful.

"Gratitude changes the giver."

— **Eric Mosley**, co-founder and CEO of Workhuman

THANK-U:
The six buildings blocks your thank-you letter needs

"You're always thanking donors – but as a donor, without your hard work and dedication my money is worth nothing. It's only money, you guys translate it into *love*."

— **Letter from 'Clara,'** *a real-life donor who has confirmed a legacy pledge in her will*

Thanks to the good and generous people around the globe who give of their money and time, nonprofits are able to do some of the most heroic, urgent, inspiring, essential work on earth.

That's no secret to either one of us.

So I ask you.

Given such urgent-inspiring-essential work and the people who support it, why would <u>anyone</u> want to begin a thank-you letter with:

On behalf of the board of directors, the CEO, and all twenty-seven trustees of our core executive leadership team, we would like to acknowledge your recent contribution [...]

Why open with <u>that</u> for a thank-you letter, when instead they could start with something like this[1]:

Dear <<formalsalu>>,

Robots whir. Comets streak. Tide pools gurgle. When science comes to life, anything is possible... and all because of you.

Thank you for your contribution of $<<trcptamt>> in support of the Ontario Science Centre! Your gift is already inspiring a generation of future scientists and their families who, without

---

Or this:

You saved a life today. Really, you did. And I just want to say thank you, from my heart to yours.

Your thank-yous can (and must!) feel as wonderful to donors as *"anything is possible... and all because of <u>you</u>"* or *"You saved a life today,"* every time.

Sure, you can use generative AI like ChatGPT to get you over writer's block. Or (*maaaybe*) with a rough draft assist. But it's a tool. You have to know the quality of what you get back. I say it's **more than okay** if you prefer to craft the right words on your own. I do. Heart and humanity still matter.

Even if you're a one-person team, or part of a bootstrapping fundraising shop with zero budget to outsource, you don't have to default to "on behalf of" boilerplate. You <u>can</u> master the skills for doing an all-star job of thanking donors all on your own.

---

1 "Sample Thank-you letters for You To Swipe," by Lisa Sargent, for The Showcase of Fundraising Innovation and Inspiration (SOFII), https://sofii.org/article/sample-thank-you-letters-for-you-to-swipe.

**It all starts when you learn how to apply
six, simple building blocks that are essential to
almost every thank-you letter you'll ever write.**

Let's begin with the thank-you letter, featured at right in its entirety, that uses all six building blocks. You don't have to dissect the letter. Just read it. How the words sound. How the letter makes you feel in your heart.

Now picture each of the six building blocks as a brief paragraph, or even just a sentence or two. You'll add them, in different ways, to the thank-you letters you write.

There are other qualities your thank-you letter will need, mind you. You'll master those in chapters to come. But for now, as long as you include these six building blocks in your thank-yous, your letter will be <u>well</u> on its way to accomplishing everything you need it to, and treating donors like the stellar human beings they are.

**The six building blocks of your essential thank-you letter
are easy to remember.**

Just think T-H-A-N-K-U...

T – **THANK** and tell the donor their gift was received – confirmation.

H – **HELP** the donor to see what their gift is doing (or will do) – justification.

A – **ASK** the donor for something <u>other</u> than money – invitation.

N – **NOTIFY** the donor how they can reach you with questions – information.

K – **KINDLE** good feelings by showing how the donor's gift is helping – illumination.

U – **UPDATE** the donor on when they'll next hear from you – expectation.

Turn to page 8 when you've finished the letter, and we'll look at each part in turn...

Postal Address
PO Box 11958,
Dublin 8

Location
24 Merchants Quay,
Dublin 8

Contact
tel: +353 (0)1 524 0139
fax: +353 (0)1 524 0946
email: info@mqi.ie
web: www.mqi.ie

MQI

Merchants Quay Ireland

A hot meal. A helping hand. A fresh start.

Title Surname
Address 1
Address 2
Address 3
Address 4
Address 5

DATE

Dear <<Salutation>>,

He cast one last look over his shoulder at MQI as he walked away, and he smiled at us. "Thanks a million," he said.

His body and clothes were clean. His hunger and thirst, quenched. And on his freshly tended and bandaged feet?

He wore new socks and sturdy shoes. *Thanks a million, he said.*

There is no way I can ever sufficiently thank you for your kind summertime donation of €<<Gift Amount>> to Merchants Quay Ireland...

... No way I can ever express what it means for me to be able to write you for urgent help with simple things like food and fresh water and clean socks and shoes and safe shelter, and know that you – forever cherished, within our Merchants Quay family – will somehow come through.

Even in summer, the unlikeliest of seasons. Thank you.

If you have chosen to receive it, your *Quay Times* donor newsletter will continue to reach you via post, with stories of the good work you so kindly make possible. Meanwhile you are very welcome to call us with any queries you might have. We are here for you.

May you find a peaceful patch of shade to call your own this summer in return for sharing life's great blessings with those in need,

[SIGNATURE]

Tony Geoghegan
CEO, Merchants Quay Ireland

P.S. You are our heart and soul, whether you give often or you have a few lean years. And to honour the grace you bring, I cordially invite you to Coffee Mornings at our Riverbank homeless centre. Once each month we host private guided tours for you, our donors, without whom MQI wouldn't exist at all. The centre isn't in active use during those brief windows, so the tours are discreet and respect the privacy of our clients. I hope you'll join me by ringing Emma on 01 524 0139 – the next dates are XX July and XX August. Thank you again for your caring spirit.

Copywriter: Lisa Sargent | Design: Sandie Collette, S. Collette Design
Client: Merchants Quay Ireland

It's important to note that I call these six essentials "building blocks" to urge and encourage you to work with each as a plug-and-play component. Sometimes they'll be a sentence or two. Sometimes, a paragraph.

And just like those alphabet towers you built and rebuilt when you were young, when it comes to the six thank-you blocks, the order is up to you and what suits your letter best.

For example, in one letter you write, the U (Update donor when they'll next hear from you) might come before the N (Notify donor how they can contact you with questions).

Or you might put the H (Help donor to see what their gift will do) way up at the top – maybe even as part of a beautiful lead to the letter – like a little story.

Treating the content like blocks will help you keep every thank-you you write fresh, flexible, and nimble.

Let's use the thank-you letter from the start of this chapter to examine each building block in turn:

T – **Thank and tell the donor their gift was received (confirmation).** If the thank-you is for a specific purpose, such as a gift to stock your summer camp's medical supplies, say that. Include the amount, if that's your policy (I do this for my clients so that the letter serves as a gift receipt too, and we've had no complaints from donors).

> There is no way I can ever sufficiently thank you for your kind summertime donation of €<<Gift Amount>> to Merchants Quay Ireland…

H – **Help the donor see what their gift is doing, or will do (justification).** When I say the gift was received and how much it was, I add a brief phrase stating what it is doing or, far more likely, <u>will</u> do. Since the thank-you is sent within 48 to around 72 hours (read Chapter 15 to explore why), if you report back to the donor on what the gift has already done, it will ring false.

> His body and clothes were clean. His hunger and thirst, quenched. And on his freshly tended and bandaged feet?
>
> He wore new socks and sturdy shoes. *Thanks a million, he said.*

A – **Ask the donor for something <u>other</u> than money (invitation).**
Invite the donor to a tour, to visit your shelter or school or sanctuary, anything relevant and supporter-centric that you can absolutely honor.

> P.S. You are our heart and soul, whether you give often or you have a few lean years. And to honour the grace you bring, I cordially invite you to Coffee Mornings at our Riverbank homeless centre. <u>Once each month we host private guided tours for you, our donors, without whom MQI wouldn't exist at all</u>. <u>The centre isn't in active use during those brief windows</u>, so the tours are discreet and respect the privacy of our clients. I hope you'll join me by ringing Emma on 01 524 0139 – the next dates are XX July and XX August. Thank you again for your caring spirit.

Another idea is to mention the notion of legacy – but do so gently to existing donors, and <u>only</u> if you have a legacy information packet you can promptly mail in response, and/or a knowledgeable staff person dedicated to this purpose, or some friendly, credible information around bequests on your website. (Find two legacy possibilities in the list on page 160.) The goal here is to provide an extra opportunity to engage, <u>not</u> to close a deal.

N – **Notify the donor how they can reach you if they have questions (information).**
This means a phone number that will be answered by staff that have been properly trained on answering donor calls, and know who to refer donors to if there are further questions.

> If you have chosen to receive it, your *Quay Times* donor newsletter will continue to reach you via post, with stories of the good work you so kindly make possible. Meanwhile you are very welcome to call us with any queries you might have. We are here for you.

You'll note in the above example that I didn't include the phone number – this is because a number and name to call appears in the postscript.

K – **Kindle good feelings by describing how the gift is helping in <u>human</u>, <u>emotional</u>, <u>inspiring</u> ways (illumination).**

Below are two examples, with more in the letters and snippets sprinkled throughout this book. Here your goal is to bring donors into the amazing work they're making possible, without turning it into a 5-page novel. Short and sweet is the key, and make sure it includes a reference to what they donated to in the appeal that generated the gift.

> ... No way I can ever express what it means for me to be able to write you for urgent help with simple things like food and fresh water and clean socks and shoes and safe shelter, and know that you – forever cherished, within our Merchants Quay family – will somehow come through.
>
> Even in summer, the unlikeliest of seasons. Thank you.

And the lead paragraphs which you saw earlier:

> He cast one last look over his shoulder at MQI as he walked away, and he smiled at us. "Thanks a million," he said.
>
> His body and clothes were clean. His hunger and thirst, quenched. And on his freshly tended and bandaged feet?
>
> He wore new socks and sturdy shoes. *Thanks a million, he said.*

U – **Update the donor on when they will next hear from you (expectation).**

All of my clients dependably mail donor newsletters, and most send regular enewsletters. We establish expectation, reliability, and consistency this way.

And for the record, having both a direct mail and email donor newsletter is by far the best option. But if you don't yet have either of those, you need to say something different. So if all you can do for now is to mention your website and Facebook updates for supporters, do that. (See page 159 for a PS that handles the no-newsletter update.)

Below is a sample of an update paragraph for a nonprofit that mails a donor newsletter:

> If you have chosen to receive it, your *Quay Times* donor newsletter will continue to reach you via post, with stories of the good work you so kindly make possible. Meanwhile you ▮▮▮ ▮ery welcome to call us with any queries you might have. We are here fo▮ ▮▮▮.

And here's a sample for a nonprofit that doesn't mail a newsletter:

> P.S. We post updates the moment they happen on our Facebook page, so be sure to follow ▮▮▮▮▮ for the latest updates on elephants and on all you make possible for the animals. Thank you again, from all of us at ▮▮▮▮▮▮▮▮▮.

"Thank you so much for your kind words. The gratitude from those with whom you work is very humbling and I will keep all in my prayers. I am not sure if I am signed up to the newsletter and would appreciate if you could add me to the list."

— **G.H.**, a real-life donor, and her own warm words in response to a thank-you email sent for her donation

CHAPTER

CHAPTER

2

Beyond the six THANK-U blocks: Qualities to kick your thank-you letters up a notch

"The letter was joyful, imaginative, and poetic. My reaction was such that I have increased my subscription: when I looked at my bank statement I felt my donation looked puny and I could do more."

— **Email from B.B.,** *a real-life monthly donor*

Hear me now: I am <u>not</u> against formulas and templates.

But I am, and will forever be, against tepid, cookie-cutter copy and bland, boilerplate insert-name-of-your-organization-here communications.

Including thank-yous.

Every nonprofit, <u>your</u> nonprofit, has a unique story to tell!

So while the six THANK-U building blocks you learned in the previous chapter will form the backbone of your gratitude recipe, the secret ingredients – that sparkly sprinkle of pixie dust – will always be yours and yours alone.

That means the tone, voice, and pacing you establish and, as B.B. the real-life donor said, that "joyful, imaginative, and poetic" thanking will <u>always</u> belong to you. (Same goes for all your fundraising and donor stewardship communications, by the way.)

Remember this little bit of wisdom as you and I hit the ground running again with another sample of how a donor-delighting thank-you should read.

I wrote it for the hardworking Irish charity ChildVision, and it was sent to supporters who'd made a cash gift to their Christmas appeal.

<u>It remains one of my favorite thank-you letters to this day, because it encompasses nearly all the tips and techniques you're about to master</u>... just turn the page to begin!

"Do your little bit of good where you are; it's those little bits of good put together that overwhelm the world."

— Archbishop Desmond Tutu

Thank you! *Thank you!*

ChildVision
National Education Centre for Blind Children

<<Name>>
<<Sample Address1>>
<<Sample Address2>>
<<Sample Estate>>
<<Sample Town>>
<<Co. Sample>>

Date

Dear <<Salutation>>,

Second star to the right, and straight on till morning.

Your Christmas donation of <<€AMOUNT>> has given children living with sight loss and other complex disabilities the wings to soar here at ChildVision.

Teaching toys… therapy toys… triumphant toys. The magic of music… magnificent, miraculous, mobility horses. Braille books to bring bold, bright beginnings. Dazzling adaptive technology to spark independence and participation in a sighted world.

Gifts of a lifetime, all. And all thanks to you.

Here at ChildVision you are the song in our hearts and the star in our sky. We couldn't help children in Ireland with sight loss, without you. Thank you so very much for caring this Christmas.

Please know that you are always welcome to call us on 01 837 3635 with any queries you have. <u>We are happy to help you however we can.</u>

Here's to a new year filled with love, learning, and laughter,

Brian Allen

Brian Allen
CEO, ChildVision

P.S.   Unless you've requested otherwise, I'll write you in the months ahead to update you on how your generosity is touching the lives of the children here – watch for your ChildVision *Member Newsletter* coming in spring. Until then, in return for the great love you have shown to every student here, thank you. And may all your wishes come true in the new year.

ChildVision, Grace Park Road, Drumcondra, Dublin 9
T 01 837 3635   **E** info@ChildVision.ie   **W** www.ChildVision.ie

Directors: Shane Cowley (Chairperson), David Myers, Monica Leech, Dan Browne, Michael O'Shea, Christopher Cassedy, Josephs O'Reilly, Michael Monaghan, Richard Ryan, Marian Harte
Registered in Dublin, No 453711, CHY817

Copywriter: Lisa Sargent | Design: Sandie Collette, S. Collette Design | Client: ChildVision
Why the magenta? Short answer: Designer Sandie and I use magenta fields to denote that these are variable (merge) fields and will use data supplied by client.

**What qualities, specifically, does this thank-you letter possess –
and how can your thank-you capture the same?
Let's explore...**

1.) The essential thank-you letter uses donor-friendly language.

For many of you this will seem like a no-brainer. But having seen too many letters that continue to ignore the tenets of solid, donor-centered, we-give-a-damn-about-you language, I'm including a mini-lesson.

Language you should choose when crafting your thank-you is:
- ♥ **Plainspoken**
- ♥ **Human**
- ♥ **Warm**
- ♥ **Genuine**
- ♥ **Heartfelt**
- ♥ **Simple**
- ♥ **You-focused** (with the occasional "I" of the writer, and/or Together We, as in you and me: "Together, we will save Earth's last mountain gorillas.")

Language to avoid at all costs is:
- ✗ **Jargon/corporate/buzzwordy** ("Paradigm," "synergy," "facilitating," "stakeholder," and the like. Don't get me started.)
- ✗ **Boilerplate/cookie cutter**
- ✗ **Self-impressed** (focused only on your organization, your accomplishments, and mostly ignores the donor)
- ✗ **Royal We, as opposed to Together/Community We** (as in "This year, we have preserved 7,000 acres of cloud forest. We have established a cutting-edge education program. We reach underserved populations. We are facilitating a paradigm shift *blah blah blah*...." My eyes glaze over: it's Royal We that distances you from your donors.)

**A word about words like *programs... services...*
and *food insecure*:**

You may have read somewhere that words like "programs" and "services" are internal jargon – hence, taboo.

<u>This is complete and total rubbish in my experience</u>.

In properly crafted donor communications, including in appeals and thank-yous, words like *programs*, *projects*, and *services* work just fine.

Avoiding them forces you to substitute less-clear phrases, wasting a wagonload of words that don't need wasting.

**The key words here are *properly crafted* –
and I'll give you an example of what that looks like,
thankologist-style.**

Just below is my rewrite of a thank-you letter as part of my free Donor Thank-you Clinics on the stupendous online resource that is **SOFII.org**. In this letter, the UK-based conservation trust (referred to in the example as XYZ Charity) asked to remain anonymous for the clinics so their before-and-after thank-you letters could be shared for the benefit of all.

Note the open and honest use of language around programs (programmes) and services, and how they connect back to the donor and to protecting the natural environment[2]:

«Salutation»,

They flit from flower to flower. Trundle across dune heaths. Glisten in the grass. Each butterfly, beetle and bee orchid, protected because of you.

And on your anniversary of joining XYZ Charity, I'd like to thank you. Through your <<frequency>> direct debits of <<amount>>, you protect the countryside we love – and the creatures who live here.

As a member of XYZ Charity, you support the nature programmes that inspire young environmentalists... advocacy teams that speak out for our region's rare wildlife species... outreach services that teach local businesses how to thrive while caring for nature, and more.

We'll be sure to keep you updated on how you're helping – from heath to hillside – in our annual newsletter, and in *Our Magazine*, the XYZ Charity magazine that's free to members. And arriving shortly, you'll also receive your tax-deductible receipt and direct debit update form.

Copywriter: Lisa Sargent | Featured on: SOFII (sofii.org)

---

2   "Sample thank-you letters for you to swipe," Lisa Sargent's free Thank-you Clinics on the Showcase of Fundraising Innovation and Inspiration (SOFII), https://sofii.org/article/sample-thank-you-letters-for-you-to-swipe. Last accessed: April 18, 2024.

And here's one more rewrite from my Donor Thank-you Clinics on SOFII that livens up words like *research projects and studies*, from the wonderful Menzies Research Institute, Tasmania, Australia:

---

18 April 2024

Dear «Salutation»

Phillip and Peter have lived with crippling arthritis since they were teens. But today, thanks to you, they have hope. Hope that one day a cure can be found.

And if hope is at the heart of our research, you are surely at the heart of Menzies – making possible each new discovery, each breakthrough treatment. Thank you for your generous donation of «GrossTotal» to the Menzies Research Institute, and welcome!

Your gift is already working to make life better for those with severe arthritis, through trailblazing research and volunteer-based studies now underway at Menzies. And by standing behind every Menzies scientist – who searches for clues to everything from diabetes to cancer – you bring hope and healing to people who live with these diseases, across Tasmania and beyond.

As a vital part of the Tasmanian community, you are vital to the work of Menzies. And I'm eager to share each new success with you in your supporter newsletter, *The Bulletin*.

In the meantime, you'll find enclosed a receipt for your tax-deductible donation. Please feel free to ring me if you have any questions about Menzies research, on 00 0000 0000. I'd love to hear from you.

On behalf of everyone here at the Menzies Research Institute, thank you for supporting the future of healing.

Yours sincerely

[insert signature]

NAME
Director

P.S. On our website at www.menzies.utas.edu.au, you'll find updates on more than 100 research projects, such as those focused on osteoarthritis, heart disease and cystic fibrosis. I hope you'll visit the site soon, and thanks again for giving.

Copywriter: Lisa Sargent | Featured on: SOFII (sofii.org)

You now know that, used properly, words like *programs, projects,* and *services* make the cut.

However.

Phrases like "underserved," "food insecure," and "hydration challenged" MUST go. They are not your friends, delete them.

Say what you mean instead. Say what <u>donors</u> understand.

Food insecure, to the vast majority of us, means hunger. Or acutely malnourished (but only if that's true).

Hydration challenged is thirsty. Or people who are suffering without access to safe, disease-free water.

Underserved are people who for whatever reason can't access or are denied access to the help they need. People being excluded from society. Families who've somehow fallen through the cracks. Off the radar.

Yes, it makes for longer copy.

But in this case, the words aren't wasted. Not by a long shot. Because you're saying the bravest, truest thing you can – and saying what donors understand.

The faceless, jargonese "Underserved" serves no one.

If my gift helped mothers and fathers to feed their families who would otherwise have gone hungry, for the love of all that is right and good in this world, <u>say so</u>!

You are in no way demeaning anyone to say: your kind gift will bring much-needed, nourishing food "to hardworking people who don't have enough to eat right here at home," or "to families who wouldn't be able to have a Thanksgiving dinner if not for your help."

2.) The essential thank-you letter considers the audience.

This is a hard and fast rule: <u>remember who you're writing to</u>.

By this I mean that at the vast majority of charities, the vast majority of donors are older.

Like 65-years-and-up older.

So when you write a thank-you about your food drive to help neighbors whose kids don't get enough to eat, don't try to sound hip or cute or clever by using weird, dissonant phrases that not only diminish the severity of what beneficiaries face, but that your 85-year-old auntie wouldn't understand. (Phrases like "Jazz hands!" and "Touchdown dance!" spring immediately to mind.)

Think I'm being hopelessly outdated and uncool with this one?

Think again: at one charity, donors – and not just one or two – complained about the use of the word *kids* instead of *children*. We now solely say *children*.

So... unless you are a woman at least 65 years old who uses cheaters to read regular print and has increasing difficulty discerning subtle differences in color and tone... chances are, you are <u>NOT</u> your donors. Not even close.

3.) The essential thank-you letter uses acronyms with care.

You <u>must</u> use acronyms with care.

That means if you are the North American Association for Kittens in Need, you can't just plop NAAFKIN into your thank-you three or four times with no explanation.

It reads like donor kryptonite, for one thing.

For another, your acronym almost certainly is not instantly identifiable to most people.

You <u>must</u> make it clear, every time. Even to existing donors.

The International Rescue Committee, as just one example, uses its IRC acronym across all of its donor communications.

At nearly one billion dollars in revenue as of fiscal year-end 2021, this is no small charity. And they've been responding to some of the world's worst humanitarian crises since 1933, when Albert Einstein inspired the organization's founding.

Still, if you follow the IRC online, you'll find that even after all these years they almost never use their acronym solely. Instead, they use <u>both</u> the International Rescue Committee name in full and the IRC acronym in the copy, because that's what donors know.

If you were doing this for your own organization, the general guideline is to use the full name and the acronym together one time, for clarity. Like this:

Your Charity Name Here (YCNH)

THEN you interchange, using only the full name or only the acronym throughout the article or appeal. And, you do this more than once, <u>because you can't guarantee that anyone will read what you write in a linear fashion, ever</u>. Trust me on this one please.

Using this acronym/name strategy also serves the dual purpose of reinforcing your nonprofit's full name in the minds of your donors – just don't overdo it.

4.) The essential thank-you letter applies good tone and pacing.

No matter what kind of fundraising writing you are doing, your tone needs to be personal, intimate, genuine, authentic, and real.

<u>Especially</u> with thank-yous.

This is a heartfelt letter of appreciation from one person to another! The tone of your thank-you – the general ambiance or feeling you create – <u>must be human first</u>.

By that I mean you <u>avoid</u> dry, sterile, pompous, academic language.

Your tone also needs to be mostly positive. This is a thank-you: you want to infuse it with emotion, of course. But now is <u>not</u> the time to sound like an appeal.

As to pacing – the rate at which your letter reads, ebbs, and flows – think simple. Mostly simple sentences. Mostly shortish paragraphs.

5.) The essential thank-you letter attends to the letterhead.

At some organizations the letterhead itself is so institutional and so off-putting that I now request to see a letterhead sample before writing.

And I mean before writing *<u>anything</u>*: whether it's a new client's thank-yous or appeals or newsletter cover letters, even.

In advance of all that I tell clients we might need to friendly it up, and why.

By way of example, one letterhead I was shown consisted of a dark green, <u>two-inch wide</u> right sidebar that ran down the entire length of the first page.

It gets worse.

In 8-point (read as: why hello I am tiny eight-point font)...

Reversed-out type (read as: reversed-out is white type on a dark background)...

They listed all *twenty-plus* members of the board.

Do not let something as simple as your standard letterhead be a wrecking ball to that intoxicating brain-chemical bath of serotonin, dopamine, and oxytocin that science has proven you can spark with gratitude. (Want more on this? See page 134.)

For the record, my designer Sandie and I often move the board members or executive leadership – if it's a requirement that they be listed – to a footer at the bottom of a page. Smaller, and apart from the letter. But not in 8-point type. And not reversed out.

6.) The essential thank-you letter defeats dehumanizing details.

By defeating dehumanizing details I mean one thing, mostly.

The ubiquitous Donor ID code that organizations add near or beside the address block, looking something like this:

Donor ID: 231957

A giant donor ID code does NOT in any way, shape, or form tell me that I matter to your nonprofit! Instead it makes me a faceless number in a sea of numbers. We get enough of that dehumanizing nonsense in our day-to-day lives, and no one (seriously, no one) wants more.

If you absolutely must use an ID on the thank-you letter, possibly for coding your address block, at least tuck it somewhere unobtrusive.

Another dehumanizer is often found in your letterhead: the *info@* prefix in the email reply address line of your organization's address and contact information.

Even worse is *admin@*. Or – I've seen it – *webmaster@*.

As thankologists, you and I can do better.

Here's how...

Change *info@* to something that reinforces how much you care about donors, <u>and</u> how important their queries and feedback are to you. Try:

- ♥ *supportercare@*
- ♥ *membercare@*
- ♥ *donorcare@*
- ♥ or even *hello@* – still friendlier than "info" or "admin"!

Here's an example of the wonderful Vail Valley Foundation's letterhead, where you can see *supportercare@* firmly in place, and magnified for you here:

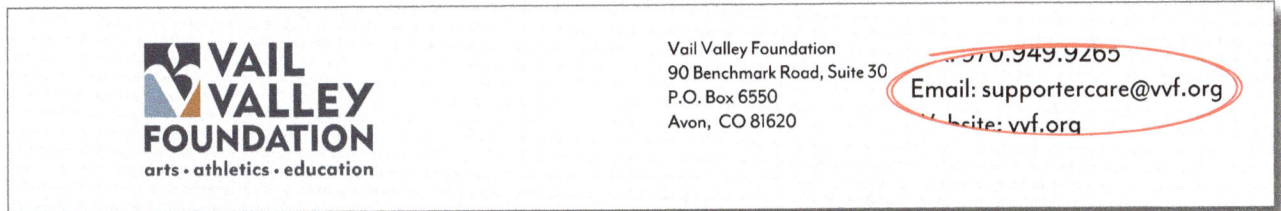

7.) The essential thank-you letter respects the rules of readability.

There's loads written on readability and reading ease.

That's because they matter a lot.

The basic guideline is this: Keep your writing somewhere between a Grade 4 and a Grade 7 (US) reading level, because people read longer (*persistence*), understand better (*comprehension*), and remember more (*retention*) when they don't have to work hard to read your copy. And if the commercial world is any indication, people also enjoy an easier read a whole lot more: some of the planet's best-selling authors write in this same range[3].

It's important to note that this works at any organization, including when handling really complex topics like medical technology and life-saving surgical techniques. In a study of my own fundraising appeals, I discovered that the best performers all hold reading levels between Grade 4 and Grade 6[4].

Reader-friendly reigns supreme. Just don't go below Grade 4 – it becomes a bit <u>too</u> elementary at that point.

So how can you figure out where your writing stands?

---

3 Snow, Shane. "*What Reading Level Should You Write At?*". [online] https://shanesnow.com/research/data-reveals-what-reading-level-you-should-write-at/ Last accessed: July 24, 2024.

4 Personal note: below Grade 4 I've found the writing becomes overly simple and feels choppy and stilted. You may want to experiment. But bottom threshold for me is Grade 4.

Hemingway Editor is one of my favorite ways, because it's free, fast, and easy to check for jargon, difficult to read sentences, and reading level. All you have to do is paste in your copy and it gives you back your stats.

I use Hemingway almost daily, and you can find it at https://hemingwayapp.com.

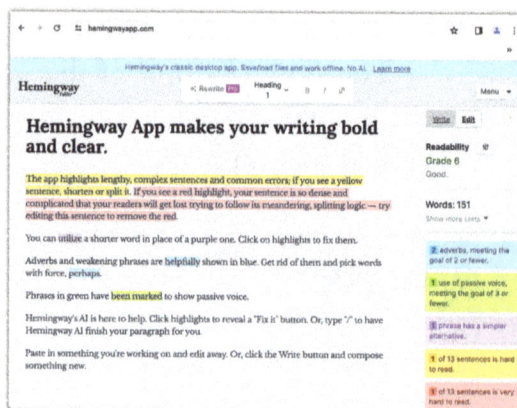

Other readability scoring systems include Flesch-Kincaid, Gunning Fog, and Fry Graph.

8.) The essential thank-you letter looks after *page architecture*.

All of my thank-you letters are one page, one side.

That means you can hold them in your hand, never flip the page, and read the whole, warm, welcoming thing.

This is not to say you couldn't test a 2-sided thank-you.

But beware: a thank-you is special.

You don't want to fall in love with your words until it looks so much like an appeal that donors mistake it for a fundraising letter.

If anything, I'd test shorter first: including, when appropriate, a handwritten thank-you card.

Page architecture, in my and Designer Sandie's world, means the structure of the page itself: if you hold it at arm's length, what do you see? The daunting Wall of Type, or loads of lovely white space and easy to follow formatting? *Page architecture.*

For direct mail, this means I tab my paragraphs, use at least one-inch margins, never less than 12-14 point serif font (or a typeface that sets similarly) with hard returns between paragraphs (meaning we don't squish up the space after a paragraph).

Applying the aforementioned formatting gives your reader lots of breathing room, like when you have a beautiful walking path all to yourself: no rush, loads of time to explore and take it all in.

To illustrate page architecture in the extreme, and note that to better illustrate for you, I'm using appeals here not thank-you letters: let's analyze the page architecture of the two letters below.

The letter on the **right** has a "modified block style" for page architecture (tiny paragraph tabs, no hard returns between paragraphs, right-justified margin). And sadly you and I have both seen these kinds of letters used in donor communications: daunting.

The letter on the **left**, though, has the page architecture you and I will use. Tabbed paras, ragged right margin, hard returns, etc. And lots of "air" – what we writers call *white space* – to rest the eyes, guide the eyes, and draw the reader in:

Generally there are no embedded photos in my thank-yous because I want to preserve that intimate, personal tone and feel. But yours could absolutely have a photo, lots of wonderful thank-yous do.

9.) The essential thank-you letter makes it personal.

The salutation on your thank-you should be personalized, as in "Dear Alice," for example, or "Dear Mr. and Dr. Jones." (Tip: if you know the donors, and are <u>100% certain</u> you have the correct info, you can cross off a "Mr. and Mrs." or a "Ms." salutation and handwrite their first names.)

And double check your data.

If you send "Dear Alicia," to a "Dear Alice," – or Mrs. Jones when it's Ms. or Dr. – that's a strike against you.

A strike that just might cost you a donor.

10.) The essential thank-you letter (almost always) opens with one or two lead sentences <u>other</u> than thank you... and <u>NEVER</u> (ever!) with *"On behalf of."*

Understand this.

Short of no thank-you at all, there is nothing on this earth that screams we are a faceless-organization-that-distances-ourselves-from-donors faster than the words *On behalf of* or *On behalf of the Board of trustees and executive leadership.*

Your goal as a thankologist is to write copy that attracts, invites, and inspires, and there are far better ways to do that than "on behalf of."

Need examples?

<u>Here are ten thank-you letter leads I've written, short and not-so-short</u>:

- 🧡 What a remarkable thing you have done.
- 🧡 You, wonderful you.
- 🧡 Gratitude. Generosity. Kindness. Love.
- 🧡 There is no easy way to say thank you for giving someone back their future... their life.
- 🧡 She stood alone by the side of the road... and *you were there*. She cried for help... and *you were there*. She longed for freedom... and *you were there*.
- 🧡 What can a child with blindness <u>really</u> do? The sky's the limit, because of you...
- 🧡 It's been said if the only prayer you ever speak is thank you, that will be enough.
- 🧡 Half a world away, a boy and a veterinarian huddle together at the roadside. They don't even speak a common language. But today they work side by side, barely a breath apart.
- 🧡 You changed someone's life this winter. Really, you did...
- 🧡 Stronger together, no matter what.

Throughout this book you'll see more leads to get you writing... until that day when you have your own handcrafted list of lovely thank-you leads. Specific to your cause. Your clients. Your work.

And none of those leads will start with the words "On behalf of..."

"You just know when charities are good charities by the way they follow up on things. Not coming back makes me feel – oh. Did they get my [donation]?"

— **Real-life donor feedback (more in Part IV)**

Sweating the small stuff:
Dead simple rules on signatories, postscripts, and donor thank-you disclaimers

> "Welding a JCB [excavator] to a Ferrari doesn't make a machine that can dig roads at 200 mph. It makes something that doesn't do either job properly."
>
> — **Dave Trott,** *Predatory Thinking*

Whenever I train, teach, or speak on the subject of donor thank-yous, or audit them for others, one thing holds fast: the littlest details cause the largest roadblocks.

With furrowed brows and frustrated eyes, fundraisers ask me —

We're required to put in a tax disclaimer... what the heck do we <u>do</u> with it?

There are <u>three</u> founders of our organization... can my thank-you be from all three of them?

There's another charity in town that uses a P.S. in its thank-you letters... why are they bothering to do that? Should we?

If one of these frustrated fundraisers is you, I understand completely.

You'll be rolling along with a beautiful thank-you nearly finished when suddenly you realize... TAX DISCLAIMER. Required text. Legalese.

Ugh.

Way to kill the warm glow of giving, right?

Well, here's the thing: <u>you're 100% right to sweat the small stuff</u>! All of the best thank-you letters do.

And, more good news!

There are simple rules to respect those devilish details, AND keep the joy of generosity and gratitude shining bright as the North Star in your letter.

Here are a few of the most common stumbling blocks in thank-yous, and how to overcome them...

Postscripts (a.k.a. the PS): The simple rule on postscripts in your thank-yous is, <u>use them</u>.

Yes, even in your email thank-yous to donors.

In fact, I want you to go so far as to picture your thank-you postscripts as the sweet, golden glitter on your gratitude cake.

Why?

Because your reader's eye LOVES the PS!

So much so that in Siegfried Vögele's legendary *Handbook of Direct Mail: The Dialogue Method of Direct Communication*, his eye-tracking studies showed <u>more than nine out of ten readers read your postscript first</u>.

Signatories (a.k.a. who signs your letter): The simple rule on signatories is, choose ONE... with the right title. And I beg you: aim for a sign-off sweeter than "Sincerely."

_If_ you have multiple people of equal prominence – like the three-founder dilemma at the start of this chapter – choose just one to be your signatory whenever possible.

Whoever you choose, make it come from the top. Your donors are <u>that</u> important!

This means a letter from the leader of your organization, or the appeal signatory if it was a special campaign. CEO, Executive Director, President – these are all terrific choices for who should sign your donor thank-you letters.

Also: beware of titles that alienate or confuse.

Let's say an organization decides to use the Assistant Director of Advanced Individual Philanthropic Giving to sign donor thank-you letters.

Well. To your nonprofit staff, that job title might mean something.

To your donors, though? It's a title that says something completely different.

Such as: "we are using your donations for lofty-sounding titles." Which leads to: "we pay a bunch of extraneous staff so less of your gift helps the cause."

I'm not saying either of these things is true, mind you. That's not the point.

<u>The point is what your donors might _perceive_</u>.

A lofty-sounding job title is also confusing because, almost always, supporters usually have no idea what it means. The end result is that their perception of how much they, and their gifts, matter is diminished.

One last note: if you are writing a thank-you to a major donor who has an established relationship with one of your major donor staff, it's possible that staff person will be the signatory. Same goes with legacy communications, so please think critically about this each and every time.

> ✓ **Signatories (a.k.a. who signs your letter): The *general* rule on signatories is, choose ONE... with the right title.**
> **[Note *general*: might a team sign a card? Yes.]**

This is not to say that *Sincerely* is bad or disrespectful or improper. It isn't.

But it's ordinary. Expected. Predictable. The equivalent of autopilot.

So instead of *Sincerely*, why not use the sign-off to really *say* something? To further surprise, delight, inspire, or uplift?

Here are four sign-off examples to try on for size:

- ♥ [Animal rescue] Until <u>every</u> dog and cat finds their forever home,
- ♥ [Human rights] Thank you again for fighting the good fight,
- ♥ [Reinforce need] This work wouldn't be possible without you,
- ♥ [Medical research] Thank you again for every miracle you make,

You see what I mean.

> ✓ **Nonprofit status and tax deductibility disclaimers:**
> **The simple rule is, don't make them microscopic.**

As of this book's writing, without digging too deep into tax law, US tax reform has made it so that it's no longer beneficial for many tax filers to take advantage of the tax deductibility of charitable donations.

That said, your nonprofit may still require adding a nonprofit status and deductibility disclaimer to your donor thank-you letters.

I've heard countless fundraisers say it's best to bury this often-cumbersome language in a quiet corner of the thank-you. Like on the back of the reply envelope, or in tiny text on the back side of the letter. Or to secret it away somewhere else altogether.

Confession? I've been including them in the footer of the letter since forever. Better yet, when warmly and clearly worded and not hidden away like an embarrassment, they read just fine.

If you're required to include this kind of language in your thank-yous, you can do the same by borrowing from, or adapting, one of the examples below.

Word to the wise.

<u>Any</u> legal disclaimer or nonprofit status disclosure needs to be fully vetted and approved by your attorneys or your legal team, <u>*including* any use or adaptation of the samples I offer up here</u>, before you make them your own.

That out of the way, here are several I've used:

<u>Generic</u>:

Please keep this letter as your tax receipt. It affirms that << Name of Nonprofit>> is a registered 501(c)(3) organization with the Tax ID <<Tax ID number>> and that no goods or services were provided in exchange for your kind and generous donation, which may be deductible under IRS tax laws. Thank you!

<u>For a US hospital foundation</u>:

At <<Name of Nonprofit>> we care about the planet as deeply as we do great local medical care. So please save this letter as your official tax receipt. It affirms <<Name of Nonprofit>> is a registered 501(c)(3) nonprofit organization, and that no goods or services were exchanged in return for your kind donation, which may be deductible under IRS tax laws. Thank you!

<u>For an environmental organization</u>:

Please help keep Arizona beautiful by saving this letter as your gift receipt. It confirms no goods or services were provided in exchange for your kind donation. <<Name of Nonprofit>> is a registered 501(c)(3), so your gift may be deductible to the extent allowed by current IRS tax laws. Thank you!

<u>And one more, with a little heart. Literally</u>:

♥ To conserve resources, please keep this letter as your tax receipt. It lets you know [Name of Nonprofit] is a registered 501(c)(3) organization and that you received no goods or services in exchange for your wonderful donation, which may be deductible under current tax laws. Thanks for being there.

See?

Friendly. Warm. Gets the job done. Nothing to hide here, folks.

"What would so many people do without you. I would love to have more to give you. I cannot get over how thankful you are for the little I send – my love & good wishes to you all"

— **From T.W.,** *a real-life donor*

CHAPTER

4

Better thanking beyond the letterbox:
Online and email

> "Digital can be a window or a wall."
>
> — **Gerry McGovern**, *Founder, Customer Carewords®*

According to the most recent report from Blackbaud at time of writing, online giving in the U.S. accounts for about 11.3% of total fundraising if yours is a midsized nonprofit (total annual revenues between US$1 million and $10 million).

For large nonprofits (revenues above $10 million), that number is 11.1%. And for small organizations (below $1 million in total annual revenues), it's 17.8% percent.[5]

That means – for most nonprofits – of every hundred dollars in fundraising your organization receives, less than twenty dollars comes from online giving. (Yes, the Covid pandemic saw a spike in donations online. But based on results and tracking, what I and other fundraisers see is that a lot of it continues to be driven by direct mail. *Driving* channel and *giving* channel can be different.)

---

5 "2021 Online Giving Trends," Blackbaud Institute. [online] https://institute.blackbaud.com/charitable-giving-report/online-giving-trends/. Last accessed: April 19, 2024.

**So while online may not be
the Golden Ticket you're led to believe, it's still
a Golden Opportunity for you to do better donor thanking.**

And of the test donations that I and others have made online, I can tell you with absolute certainty: there is ample room for you to make your mark.

The best way to start is by discovering what it's <u>really</u> like to give to your organization online, *from your donor's perspective.*

<u>Which means, you make a couple of test donations</u>. It's (doubly) worthwhile to also give to several other nonprofits at the same time – what we direct response people call 'mystery shopping' – to see how they handle the process.*

This sounds like such an obvious first step to take, you probably imagine every nonprofit must do this regularly.

They do not.

That's why, when organizations call on me to review the way they thank their donors online, I <u>always</u> recommend they first make at least one cash test donation and one monthly test donation. We take screenshots of each step, and we track what the donor receives after the gift.

Most of them are thunderstruck at the results.

We often find that entire steps in the digital donation thank-you journey are missing completely (meaning donors aren't being recognized when they should be).

Since you can't fix the process if you don't know what's supposed to be there in the first place, you and I will focus on the three thank-you steps that should happen immediately after a donor gives online, steps that we often find missing or muddled during online thanking audits.

For deep learning, make sure one of your digital test donations is to charity:water. They serve up one of the best online giving experiences and donation confirmation pages I've seen[6], bar none.

The first step in your donor's online thank-you journey is the donation confirmation page.

Also known as the *thank you redirect page*, the *donation confirmation page* is the screen that pops up on your donor's computer, tablet, or phone <u>immediately</u> after they've filled out your online donation form and clicked the "donate" or "complete my donation" button.

It's also one of those pages that leads to bury-your-head-in-your-hands moments when we make test donations. Because sadly, many nonprofits don't use a donation confirmation page at all.

Or, the donor clicks the "Complete my donation" button and the web page that pops up still says things like "Please make a donation today," and "use the form below to donate." Only after all that is there tiny type with phrases like Billing Information, and the far ghastlier *Your donation has been processed.*

I'm not making this up. Below are <u>actual headlines I've seen on thank-you redirect pages</u> – moments after I'd just made a donation:

> ## Please make a donation today

> **Your donation has been processed.**

You can now begin to understand why the overall online retention rate for new, one-time donors is only 16%[7]. That's around two in ten digital donors, which means around eight of every ten first-time donors leave.

And <u>that's</u> tragic.

---

6 Other organizations, small and large, include thank-you videos on their donation confirmation pages. For an excellent write-up and superb how-to resources on this topic, see "4 Smart Ways to Use Thank You Videos in Nonprofit Fundraising," by Kerri Karvetski for Kivi Leroux Miller's Nonprofit Marketing Guide.

7 M+R. [online] https://mrbenchmarks.com/#fundraising, 2023 Benchmarks. Last accessed: April 19, 2024.

Now let's walk through a proper donation confirmation page, courtesy of the wonderful ChildVision in Ireland[8]:

By this point you are noticing several things this page accomplishes that *Your donation has been processed* does not, and that you can adapt for your own:

- 💙 **It uses an appropriate banner image and headline** for the feeling it's meant to evoke. Genuine gratitude. Joy. Kindness.

- 🧡 **It uses an uplifting and human-sounding lead sentence**, which in this case is: "Your donation has just changed the life of a child with sight loss and other complex disabilities in Ireland."

---

8 Many thanks to the amazing team at ChildVision for allowing me to share their donation confirmation page. Copywriting: Lisa Sargent. Design: Sandie Collette.

- ♥ **It says what the donor can expect next:** "Shortly via email, we'll send an official record of your incredibly kind donation." That way, you don't need the donation amount here – although you could include it if you choose.
- ♥ **It provides a real human contact** if the donor has questions.
- ♥ **It says thank you again.**
- ♥ **It connects the donor and beneficiary** by using almost all you/your (10 instances, in this case). We/us appear only twice.

Notice how much that sounds like the thank-you letter basics you've already started to master, and how it reassures the donor their gift is in good hands.

The second step in your donor's digital thank-you journey is the thank-you email you'll send them.

Pause for a moment and imagine yourself in your donor's shoes. You've been inspired to give online. You've made the donation. Experienced that first glorious glow of gratitude (see page 134 for the nerd-level neuroscience) at the donation confirmation page.

And you await an email that thanks you for your online gift.

But it never comes, because many organizations <u>never</u> send one.

It's true. And it's sad, when you remember that tepid twenty-two percent retention rate for first-year online donors (so, seventy-eight percent attrition).

Like a staircase, every step matters.

For you to write your way to email gratitude glory, you need to attend to ten key areas – some of which we covered already in Chapter 3, on sweating the small stuff. Here are more...

#1. Proper sender and subject lines.

To explore sender and subject lines, let's jump in our time machine and turn back the clock to fifteen minutes <u>after</u> I made nearly a dozen online test donations to various charities.

There were lots of thank-yous in the subject lines, which is a good thing. charity:water personalized theirs. As did the National Parks Conservation Association (last one at the bottom), a nice touch:

Donations	Mr. Holland's Opus Foundation- Thank you - Keeping Music Alive in our Schools January 19, 201	Jan 19
Deb Keller, Student Cons.	SCA Hands On: 10 Awesome Internships, Caption Contest, summer jobs and more... - Havir	Jan 19
Dan O'Neill, Mercy Corps	Deadline tomorrow! Join 236 others and have your gift matched - Double your monthly impact	Jan 19
The Nature Conservancy	Annual Report Videos -- Explore Your Connection to Nature - Trouble viewing this email? Face	Jan 19
Feeding, me (2)	Thanks to You - Forwarded message From: Feeding America - Vicki Escarra, President & CEO	Jan 19
PDF Friend	Thank you for supporting Parkinson's Disease Foundation - Thank you for your donation Parkinsor	Jan 18
The Nature Conservancy	Thank you for supporting The Nature Conservancy - The Nature Conservancy You Support Our W	Jan 18
Mercy Corps	Thank you for your gift! - Dear Lisa, Thank you for your gift of $10.00 to Mercy Corps! Your contrit	Jan 18
info	Pine Street Inn Thanks You For Your Support - Pine Street Inn Development Office 434 Harrison /	Jan 18
Network for Good	Thank you for your donation to MR HOLLANDS OPUS FOUNDATION - On behalf of the kids who	Jan 18
The Humane Society of th.	Thanks for your donation! - Dear Lisa, Thank you so much for your donation to The Humane Socle	Jan 18
CARE	Thank you for supporting CARE - Dear Lisa, Thank you for your generous donation. Your gift of $1	Jan 18
National Parks Conservat.	Thanks for your contribution, Lisa! - NPCA header Dear Lisa, Thank you for supporting the Nationa	Jan 18

The thing to keep in mind with thank-you subject lines is that you don't have to make it complicated: some variation of "Thank you" is perfectly acceptable.

People's inboxes are overflowing, so there's nothing at all wrong with making it clear that this is a thank-you for their donation. Stray too far, try to get clever, and you stand a chance of reducing the open rate.

As to sender fields (left column, above), note the one that once belonged to Pine Street Inn. If you're having trouble finding it, it's the one that reads "info."

They've since updated it to the name of their fabulous organization – <u>huge</u> round of applause for that, Pine Street! – but I'm using it here because nonprofits are still making this same mistake for their sender field. Yes, still.

Or they send with other generic labels like "Admin" and "Donations."

But now you know better. Which means <u>your</u> sender field will say a real person's name, and the name of your organization. (Note: like all things, digital best practices continue to evolve. If you're not familiar with **nextafter.com** and their free resources around all things online fundraising, have a look. They test extensively and share results. Plain text emails, for example? Worth exploring.)

#2. Personalization.

Just like we discussed for direct mail thank-you letters, by this point you know my name. So use it in the salutation of the email.

#3. Lead.

Same as direct mail, make it interesting. But remember that with email copy, you want to move even more quickly. Like this:

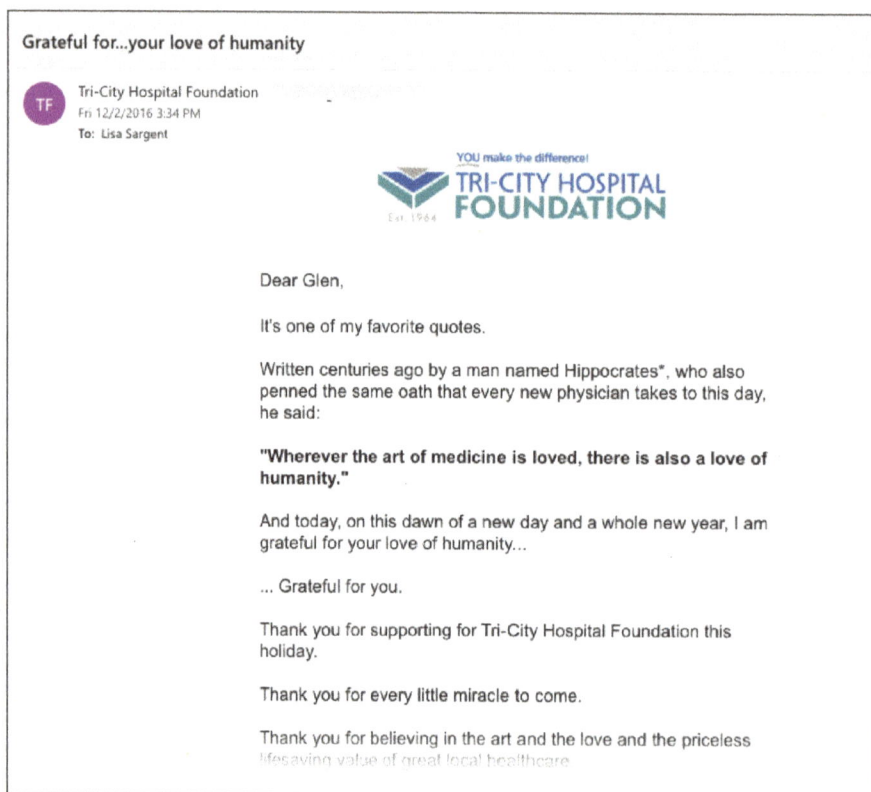

Grateful for...your love of humanity

Tri-City Hospital Foundation
Fri 12/2/2016 3:34 PM
To: Lisa Sargent

YOU make the difference!
TRI-CITY HOSPITAL FOUNDATION
Est. 1964

Dear Glen,

It's one of my favorite quotes.

Written centuries ago by a man named Hippocrates*, who also penned the same oath that every new physician takes to this day, he said:

"Wherever the art of medicine is loved, there is also a love of humanity."

And today, on this dawn of a new day and a whole new year, I am grateful for your love of humanity...

... Grateful for you.

Thank you for supporting for Tri-City Hospital Foundation this holiday.

Thank you for every little miracle to come.

Thank you for believing in the art and the love and the priceless lifesaving value of great local healthcare.

Copywriter: Lisa Sargent | Design: Sandie Collette, S. Collette Design
Client: Glen Newhart, CFRE, for Tri-City Hospital Foundation

#4. Say how the gift *will* help.

Again, this will be similar to a direct mail thank-you letter, with an important caveat: donors could be receiving your email thank-you <u>mere minutes or hours after they give</u>. This means you can't say how their gift has filled the tummies of homeless dogs and cats at your rescue, or made medical miracles happen at your hospital, because it hasn't yet.

Here's an excerpt from an email thank-you I wrote, tweaked slightly to keep the organization anonymous.

<u>Note the use of "will soon have a chance"</u>:

> They come from city pounds and puppy mills ... back alleys and small-town shelters. Still, their tender hearts hold a lifetime of love.
>
> And the homeless puppies and mother dogs who come into the care of Home Forever Animal Shelter ==will soon have a chance== to share that love with a family all their own, and all because of you!

#5. Harness email's three secret superpowers: Interactivity, Immediacy, and Instant Gratification.

Remember, with email your donor is reading from a screen, be that a cellphone, tablet, laptop, or desktop. You literally have the chance to draw them deeper into your story in seconds by inviting them to click or tap a link that delivers direct and immediate involvement.

For instant gratification, for example, charity:water sent a short and sweet thank-you email with a prominent "Watch the video >>" button. It took me to a delightful thank-you video that immersed me – sight and sound – in the great good my gift was poised to achieve. I felt connected, glad, part of something bigger than myself, and all in less than a minute or two.

Watch the video »

Another word about thank-you videos. There are companies out there that will create lovely, personalized thank-you videos for your donors. But if you're a smaller organization, you can also create your own – and there are loads of free resources to guide you[9].

When I talk about interactivity, I'm thinking of Facebook, Instagram, and other social media... plus newsletter sign-ups, and sometimes, surveys and petitions. Back at the six building blocks we talked about asking donors for something other than money in your thank-you. Imagine they donated to your appeal to protect human rights. In the postscript of your thank-you, you could thank them again for taking a stand, and invite them to add their voice to a petition you'd be bringing before lawmakers by clicking on the link you provide.

Using your email thank-you to seize and extend that moment of gratitude and engagement – using the immediacy of the digital channel to strengthen a donor's connection to your cause be it with a video or hyperlink – is absolutely worth testing.

#6. Provide the right kind of contact information. And always, an unsubscribe (know the law where you are).

Where can your donor turn if they have questions or need help?

Providing proper contact information in your email thank-you points your donor in the right direction... gets the relationship off on the

---

9 Qgiv, for example, offers up, "Use Video Thank-yous to Show Donors a Little Extra Love," https://www.qgiv.com/blog/use-video-thank-yous-to-show-donors-a-little-extra-love/, and Sandy Rees of Get Fully Funded gives you "10 Tips for Thanking Your Donors," with more helpful links at the end, https://getfullyfunded.com/10-tips-for-thanking-your-donors-with-video/. Last accessed: April, 2024.

right foot (or reinforces it) ... and puts a human face on your organization by using a warm and friendly tone.

You can keep your contact information as simple as:

> Do you have questions? We're a click or a phone call away at **donorservices@xyx.org** or [phone number here], and we'd love to hear from you.

And always provide a way for donors to unsubscribe to every email you send (again, know the law where you are: it's almost certainly required).

You can add the option in the footer at the end of your email, and keep it clear and direct. As in:

> You are receiving this email because you have previously provided [name of nonprofit] with your email address. If you'd prefer not to receive any further email from [name of nonprofit], you can unsubscribe anytime using the link at the bottom of this mail.

#7. Say when you'll be in touch next.

This rule holds as true for email as it does for direct mail: donors shouldn't have to guess if, or when, they'll get to hear how their donation is working.

After my first donation, one smart charity let me know like this (and if you're in Ireland or the UK, be mindful of GDPR requiring disclosure on the donation form):

> With your gift, you'll also become a subscriber to our email newsletter. (Rest assured, we will not sell, rent, or trade this information to a third party, and you'll be given the option to unsubscribe at the bottom of each newsletter.)

To that first sentence, you could use what you learned about the six THANK-U building blocks in Chapter 1, and connect the newsletter to the donor's recent gift, as follows:

> With your gift, you'll also become a subscriber to our monthly email newsletter, where we'll share with you all the good things your kind donation is making possible for [homeless pets, children with sight loss, the environment, etc].

If I am a new donor and you have also taken the time to craft a series of emails to welcome me to the work, you need to say this.

For two reasons.

First, if you start sending me several emails each week for a month and you only told me I'm subscribed to your monthly email newsletter, you run the risk I'll switch off and unsubscribe.

Second, more positively, is that by letting me know, you'll mentally prime me for what's coming and I'll be more likely to open and read.

In one Christmas email series I wrote, the CEO said simply, "I'll share more of our best Christmas stories with you soon." After that, each email in the series gave a heads-up to the next one and included a bit of teaser copy around the story we'd be sharing.

#8. Choose the right signatories (and signatures).

Selecting the right signatories is exactly the same for thank-you letters as for thank-you emails.

That means in most cases you'll use a single individual at or near the top of your organization, such as your CEO, Executive Director, or President. Or one of your programs staff if the gift is in response to a special appeal signed, for example, by someone working in the field (more on this in a minute).

You can use a scan of the actual signature, like with direct mail, but many organizations don't and that's perfectly fine.

One of my reigning favorites is a national animal rescue charity. In the email signature block, to the left of their CEO's (typed) name and title is a smiling thumbnail photo of him. In his arms he holds a beautiful, fluffy cat.

Instant "Awww" moment. No signature scan required.

Last thing. In your signature, include the name of the person, their title, and the name of your organization. Don't assume donors will know.

For example:

> Thank you again for being a hero to homeless pets,
> Isabella Vega
> CEO, Name of Organization

#9. Use a P.S.

Do any reading around email appeals and email thank-yous, and at some point you will come across advice urging you not to use a P.S. in your emails.

Please don't just blindly accept this.

You and I have covered the P.S. – or postscript – already, so we don't have to dig back into what you can write in them.

But know this: people <u>do</u> read email postscripts, so you should at the very least consider trying and testing them.

Clickthrough rates (the number of people who click on the link you include in your PS) of two to four percent are not unheard of, and I know because these were my clients.

Here's an effective one for homeless puppies and mama dogs [name of organization changed]:

> P.S. If you'd like to catch the latest news and videos about the rescued puppies and mama dogs you're helping, visit **www.nameoforg.org/puppypalace**. Sure to bring you a smile for the great good you do! Thanks again for giving.

#10. Attend to format, images if you use them (and their alt-tags, including for logos).

<u>Font</u>: The general rule in the past was sanserif font (or sans serif, the font families without "feet," like <u>Arial</u> and <u>Verdana</u>) for online and serif (font with feet, like Times New Roman or <u>Courier</u>) for offline. But research is mixed on the differences in comprehension. My suggestion is that if you prefer serif in your emails, make sure the f ont you choose isn't exotic – stick with a standard like <u>Times New Roman</u> – or it could default to whatever the donor's device sees as a reasonable substitute and render your well-planned message a mess.

We try to stay with <u>Arial</u>, and no smaller than 16-point font.

Yes, 16-point Arial is big. **(This big, in fact.)**

But on a small screen, it makes for <u>much</u> better reading.

And Arial is tried and true for digital, so it generally renders as you intend across most every device.

<u>Sentence, paragraph, and overall length</u>: Pacing is shorter and quicker for email. And remember, emails are narrower, so what looks like a 2-line paragraph in your word document – if you submit copy that way, like I do to Designer Sandie – can become 4 or 5 lines in an email. Aim for paragraphs of 1-3 lines, tops, and keep sentences shortish when you can. In general, we keep to 350-400 words or fewer for email thank-yous, including the PS. (Quick note: some of you will be telling me 400 words is too long. We have not seen that at all. Donors respond. And don't get me going on the "proper length" of email appeals, because that depends, too... some of my top performers hit 600 and even 700 words. Keep an open mind. Experiment. The results will surprise you.)

<u>Images and Alt-tags</u>: When you use images or graphic elements like logos, remember that a donor may be viewing them with images off or images on. If images are off, donors won't see your logo or image, but instead see a box with descriptor copy in it called an alt-tag or alt-attribute. For images especially, if you can, make that snippet of simple descriptor copy compelling enough that they want to turn on their images.

This is an example of Mercy Corps logo with images off:

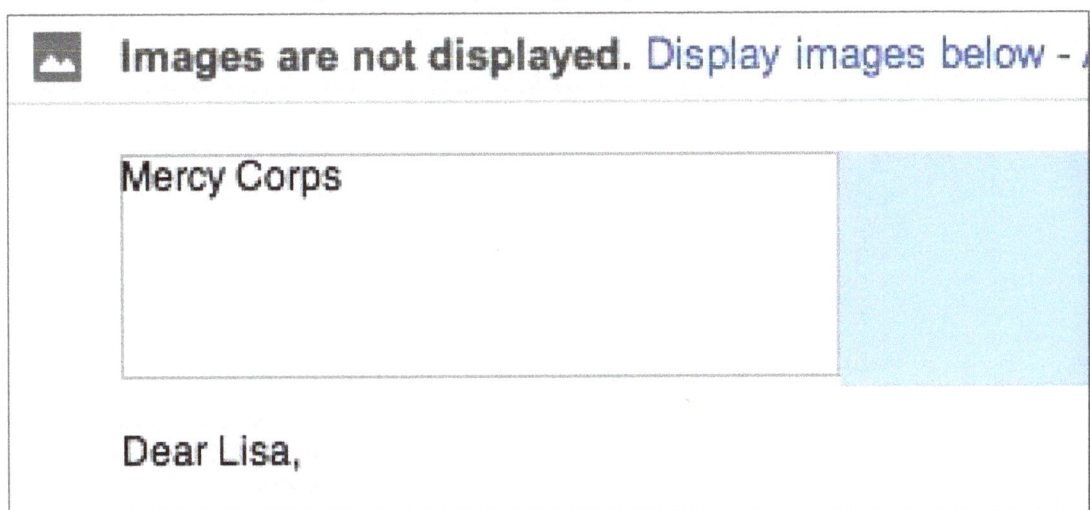

Images are not displayed. Display images below -

Mercy Corps

Dear Lisa,

Let's now move on to the final step in your digital thank-you journey.

#11.   Consider sending a direct mail thank-you letter as well.

Yes, I know this irks some of you.

However many organizations do this, my clients included, with great success. (Again, my friends in the UK and Ireland, mind your GDPR permissions please.)

What's more, the Network for Good (now Bonterra) study *Our Digital Dilemma* has proof that if you want to try the email/mail combo, you're right:

"Nonprofits that increased the number of channels used to engage donors [from one channel to 2+] retained 11.89% more donors year-over-year."

<u>Conversely, nonprofits who were using a multi-channel framework but reverted to single-channel saw their median year-over-year retention *drop* by 31.32%.</u> (A joint Virtuous/NextAfter study of 119 nonprofits showed multi-channel donors give 3X more, too.)[10]

Especially in light of all the organizations that abandon direct mail and go all digital because "it's cheaper," when you think about what that move could really cost <u>your</u> nonprofit, remember the above facts.

Let me leave you with a thank-you email I basically just assembled using the beautiful words of Trócaire's then Lent Officer (now their Individual Giving Manager), the amazing Aislinn Murphy.

Is it longer than usual? Yes. But donors loved it. In fact, they wrote back and said so:

> Lovely email Aislinn
> Thank you
> Kind regards
> Ciara

---

10 *Our Digital Dilemma*, Network for Good (now Bonterra), 2019. For Virtuous/NextAfter's 2021 study, *The State of Multi-Channel Donor Communications*, visit https://www.multichannelnonprofit.com.

Sender: Aislinn Murphy, Trócaire
Subject: Thank you for your kindness and generosity this Lent!

Dear «Informal_Salutation»,

What an honour it is to be able to write this email to you.

Thank you, from the heart of Trócaire, for your wonderful generosity and compassion in taking the time to donate <€Amount> to help incredible families like Thandekile's this Lent.

Every day as Lent Officer I have the incredible privilege of seeing your kindness in action. And I can tell you beyond a shadow of a doubt: you are bringing lasting change to the lives of people who suffer because of war, poverty, climate change, and Covid.

I hear it when I get the chance to speak with Father Innocent in Zimbabwe, and last year with Father James in South Sudan, so that I can bring you their stories. Always they share what little they have to help others, and always it's so tough when they haven't enough to help everyone who needs them.

Or ██████████, who is a teacher in the school that Thandekile's children Nomatter and Forward attend. To hear him describe what it's like to teach a class of students with hungry bellies because the rains didn't come due to climate change, you hear the pain in his voice and know his families face much tougher challenges than we do here at home to give their children a chance at tomorrow.

They are difficult conversations to have. But then I am lifted because I know that all across our island, good people with hearts for humanity like yours will never turn away. Bellies will be filled. Families will be helped. Little children, women, and men will make it through.

It's you who makes all the difference, «Informal_Salutation». You really do. Giving what you can, when you can, to help one life at a time, and together we are stronger.

Together, we can shine a light against the darkness.

Thank you so much for being our Trócaire family, this Lent and always. In the days ahead our CEO Caoimhe de Barra will send her own note of thanks for your kind gift.

For today, I just wanted to be sure and let you know that here in Ireland and around the globe, your support means the world. Please keep safe, and God bless – pray for peace, if you can.

Gratefully yours,

Aislinn Murphy
Lent Officer, Trócaire

PS. I know we thank you often for being our Trócaire family, but it really is true. Each Lent one of my favourite things is being able to read all the messages that kind people like you send in with their donations, messages for families like Thandekile's. We put them together in a book and send them to the country office, and then staff bring it out to the families to show the prayers, the gorgeous children's drawings, and the personal stories that the people of Ireland have shared. «Informal_Salutation», these messages honestly do carry so much hope – just last Lent, staff at the South Sudan office told us how much it lifted everyone's spirits to know how much everyone cared. At times when life feels at its toughest and loneliest, your loving kindness is an invisible thread of hope and humanity encircling the world. Please don't hesitate to reach out if you ever have questions, and thank you so much for taking the time to give this Lent. You bring so much strength to others.

If you receive post from Trócaire, watch for *Your Love In Action* supporter newsletter in the weeks to come with more stories of how your compassion is helping to build a better world. And if you're not sure if you're signed up to receive post, feel free to email us here. I'm so glad you're with us.

Better online and email thanking:
Your chapter recap checklist

☐ **Do you have a donation confirmation page (also known as a thank-you redirect page) that, at a minimum:**

    ☐ Does not contain any variation of "your donation has been processed" or "please give today"

    ☐ Thanks donors warmly

    ☐ Provides a real human contact, phone and email (Tip: spell out the email, don't just make it a hyperlink. That way donor can copy and paste elsewhere if needed. As in: email John at **john@abccharity.org**)

    ☐ Says what donors can expect next

☐ **Does your email thank you:**

    ☐ Use proper (human) sender and compelling subject line

    ☐ Use a personalized salutation

    ☐ Open with a short and engaging lead

    ☐ Say how the gift will help

    ☐ Provide correct contact information (see above for thank-you redirect, same rules)

    ☐ Provide an unsubscribe

    ☐ Say when you'll be in touch next

    ☐ Choose the right signatories and signatures

    ☐ Use a postscript (PS)

    ☐ Attend to font, format, images, and alt-tags

    ☐ Serve as part of a two-step process that includes a direct mail thank-you (mind your permissions here please)

    ☐ Have you made a test donation before taking everything "live," to catch any glitches or breaks in the online gratitude experience?

    ☐ If donors hit "reply" to your email, will an actual human reply to them? (Yes needs to be the answer to this.)

PART II:

Making the most of donor moments: The special purpose thank-you letters

"Transitions should be marked,
milestones commemorated, and pits filled.
That's the essence of thinking
in moments."

— **Chip Heath & Dan Heath**, *The Power of Moments*

milestone moments

Years ago, I read a story from fundraising consultant Jessica Harrington that forever changed my thoughts around thanking and communicating with donors.

She wrote of a renewal appeal that included a letter personalized to the year the donor first joined the organization and the causes it was fighting then.

It wasn't one of those insert-year-here personalizations either.

In Harrington's words:

"We didn't just pull out a date or reference a package – the customization was several paragraphs long and took the donor through the organization's history and recognizing that none of this could have happened without [the donor]."

Revenue to that renewal was up 54%[11].

Her story got me thinking about donor moments...
What can we thank donors for, and when can we thank them,
to acknowledge their milestones that we might be missing?

Best-selling authors Chip Heath and Dan Heath know a little something about *The Power of Moments*... they wrote a book by the same name.

They share the story of a personal fitness-tracking device that not only acknowledges obvious milestones, it also creates new ones for its users.

---

11   Jessica's story is shared in *Retention Fundraising*, by the wonderful Roger Craver (pg 113), and also on his must-read blog, The Agitator, in "Retention Win #1: Say Thank You," 9/9/2014, https://agitator.thedonorvoice.com/retention-win-1-say-thank-you/.

Such as:

"... the Monarch Migration Badge, which is described as follows: 'Every year the monarch butterfly migrates 2,500 miles to warmer climates. With the same lifetime miles in your pocket, you're giving those butterflies some hot competition!"[12]

Recognizing milestone moments – donor moments – can work for you, too.

I'll share an example.

One of my clients had worked hard for 25 years in a country whose people had been tragically and horrifically torn apart by violence.

In a donor newsletter, we planned to share the stories of how some of these incredible people had – against all odds and with steady support from this charity and its steadfast donors – reconciled.

Now, if you're not a thankologist, you might think in terms of the organization. "For 25 years, we have been working to reconcile," and "we implemented innovative tools" blah blah blah blah.

But we didn't say any of that.

Instead, we talked about all the amazing people who had donated all through those 25 years.

Then we went a step further: we crafted a special message for donors who'd been giving for the full 25 years.

These supporters received a special newsletter cover letter that told how it was <u>their</u> generosity that put boots on the ground in the days after the violence had only just ended...

... How it was <u>their abiding support</u> that helped lift the hearts of people who had been shattered into a thousand different pieces, and then

12 Chip Heath and Dan Heath, *The Power of Moments*, (New York, NY: Simon & Schuster, 2017), page 27.

helped them heal long after the media spotlight had moved on.

We thanked the donors, and thanked them, and thanked them some more. Then my design colleague Sandie took it another step further and created a special thank-you badge for the top of the letter (which you'll see on the sample at right).

Response rate for that segment
<u>increased 67%</u> over the prior newsletter.

Other donors were thanked abundantly too. Of course.

But the connection between the story and those 25-year supporters would have slipped by completely unnoticed – *unheralded!* – if we weren't thinking in donor moments.

Here's how that moment looked in real life – a view from the first paragraphs of the newsletter cover letter featured at right. And again, note the simple 25-year supporter badge near the top right of the letter.

In your organization's case, this means you want to: find, create, and acknowledge your donor's milestone moments.

<u>*Not*</u> the fifteenth anniversary of your founding.

<u>*Not*</u> the launch of your rebrand.

<u>*Not*</u> your organization's moments.

Your donor's moments.

How would they feel to receive a special card or letter on the one-year anniversary of their first donation?

Or to be recognized for being a supporter of your work for five, or ten, or fifty years?

What about, even, the first 100 days of their donation? (Those first 100 days matter mightily, fyi... and on page 88, we'll explore just how much more.)

trōcaire

Trócaire, Maynooth,
Co. Kildare, Ireland
Ph: (0)1 629 33 33
F: +353 (0)1 629 0661
E: donorservices@trocaire.org
www.trocaire.org

Thank you!

August 2019

<Addressee>
<Addressee Line 1>
<Addressee Line 2>
<Addressee Line 3>
<Mailing City>
<Mailing County State Province>
<Postcode>

> Next month marks twenty-five years since then president of Ireland, Mary Robinson, landed in Rwanda in 1994. She was one of the first heads of state to journey there after the horrific 100-day genocide left over one million Tutsis dead – babies, children, women, and men who were butchered in unspeakable ways. Speaking to the *Irish Times* she said, "I'll never forget the scent of blood. Children's shoes abandoned in churches."
>
> **It is hard to imagine how hope could ever follow such a seismic splintering of humanity. Hope *did* come to Rwanda, though.**
>
> Because when the world wept, you rallied to Rwandans' sides. You are still there with love and compassion today, and your enclosed newsletter tells that hero's tale. **Thank you for being a 25+ year supporter to Trócaire...**

Dear <<Name>>,

It is such an honour to write this letter to you. As a 25+ year supporter to Trócaire, you have been there for Marie ████████ from the start.

On the back of her head she bears a thick and ragged scar from the machete blow that was meant to kill her. The machete that claimed the life of her entire family.

Only Marie survived the slaughter in the church that day. One hundred such days would pass before the genocide ended in Rwanda. Over a million souls. Gone.

Copywriter: Lisa Sargent | Design: Sandie Collette, S. Collette Design
Client: Trócaire

Are there hidden donor moments that <u>you</u> can bring to light and make meaningful? That answer, thankologist, is YES!

The first-time donor thank-you letter
(And a 60-second step to consider first)

> "It's always about timing. If it's
> too soon, no one understands.
> If it's too late, everyone's forgotten."
>
> — **Dame Anna Wintour**

Walk ten steps in any direction in my neck of the New England woods, and chances are excellent you'll collide with *Quercus alba*.

One of the most important species of tree in the entire white oak family.[13]

Today its mighty planks support everything from whiskey and wine barrels to flooring and furniture, to the great sailing ships of bygone times. In the right environment *Quercus alba* lives for centuries, and can reach a height of one hundred feet. (For the rest of the world, that's 30.48 meters.)

---

13 "Field Guide to Native Oak Species of Eastern North America," J. Stein, D. Binion, R. Acciavatti, Reprinted October 2017. https://www.fs.usda.gov/foresthealth/technology/pdfs/fieldguide.pdf

But for all the white oak's amazingness and might, *Quercus alba* begins life on the wind.

The wind is how white oaks are pollinated.

The wind is how acorns, and those towering giving trees, come to be.

The whim of the wind.

When someone sends your nonprofit a donation for the first time, I want you to think of *Quercus alba*.

Born on the wind. The potential to stay and grow for years.

But fragile, to begin. In fact, that first gift?

It's a test donation. The acorn that lands, and may or may not mature.

It all depends on what you do next.

And what you do matters. A lot...

In his *Managing Donor Defection*, Professor Adrian Sargeant found that more than <u>twenty out of every hundred donors</u> who stopped giving to a charity did so because they were never thanked at all, or never informed how their donations were used (which could have happened in that thank-you letter they never got)[14].

<u>Twenty out of every hundred donors – or two donors in ten</u>.

Now remember back to the very start of this book, and Sargeant's other finding: keep just ***one*** additional donor in ten from lapsing (in other words,

---

14 The figure was 21.3%, to be exact, based on Dr. Sargeant's survey of lapsed donors at ten national nonprofits asking them, "Why did you stop giving?" and collating the results. *Managing Donor Defection*, Adrian Sargeant, https://www.onlinelibrary.wiley.com/doi/abs/10.1002/pf.3204. Excellent summary from the smart folks at Bloomerang, here: https://bloomerang.co/retention.

a ten percent increase in donor retention) and you can improve the lifetime value of your donor file by <u>two hundred percent</u>.

**There are three, potentially four, things
your thank-you letter to new donors needs to do:**

First, a reminder – these elements we're about to discuss are *in addition to* the building blocks for thank-yous that we covered in Chapters 1 and 2. Things like a warm lead, easy reading, and proper choice of signatory... all those still apply.

1. **Your first-time donor thank-you letter should welcome your
    new donor.**

    While it might not feel appropriate at this stage to welcome them to the "family," you can still warmly welcome them to the work you do.

2. **Your first-time donor thank-you letter should say what comes next.**

    Will donors receive a special welcome packet that you'll send a couple of weeks after this thank-you? Will they receive a quarterly donor newsletter, as well? In your letter you want to point the way to what's next.

3. **Your first-time donor thank-you letter should prime the relationship
    and show you'd like it to be a lasting one.**

    In the very last sentence of the postscript of the letter that follows, you'll see my gentle use of "priming," that is, exposing the donor to an idea or concept that may later influence their behavior: "I hope you're with us for many years to come." Just a simple way to say they matter, to help extend the relationship horizon, and convey that you hope they'll stay.

Here's a simple example of a new donor thank-you letter that includes all three of the points we just discussed:

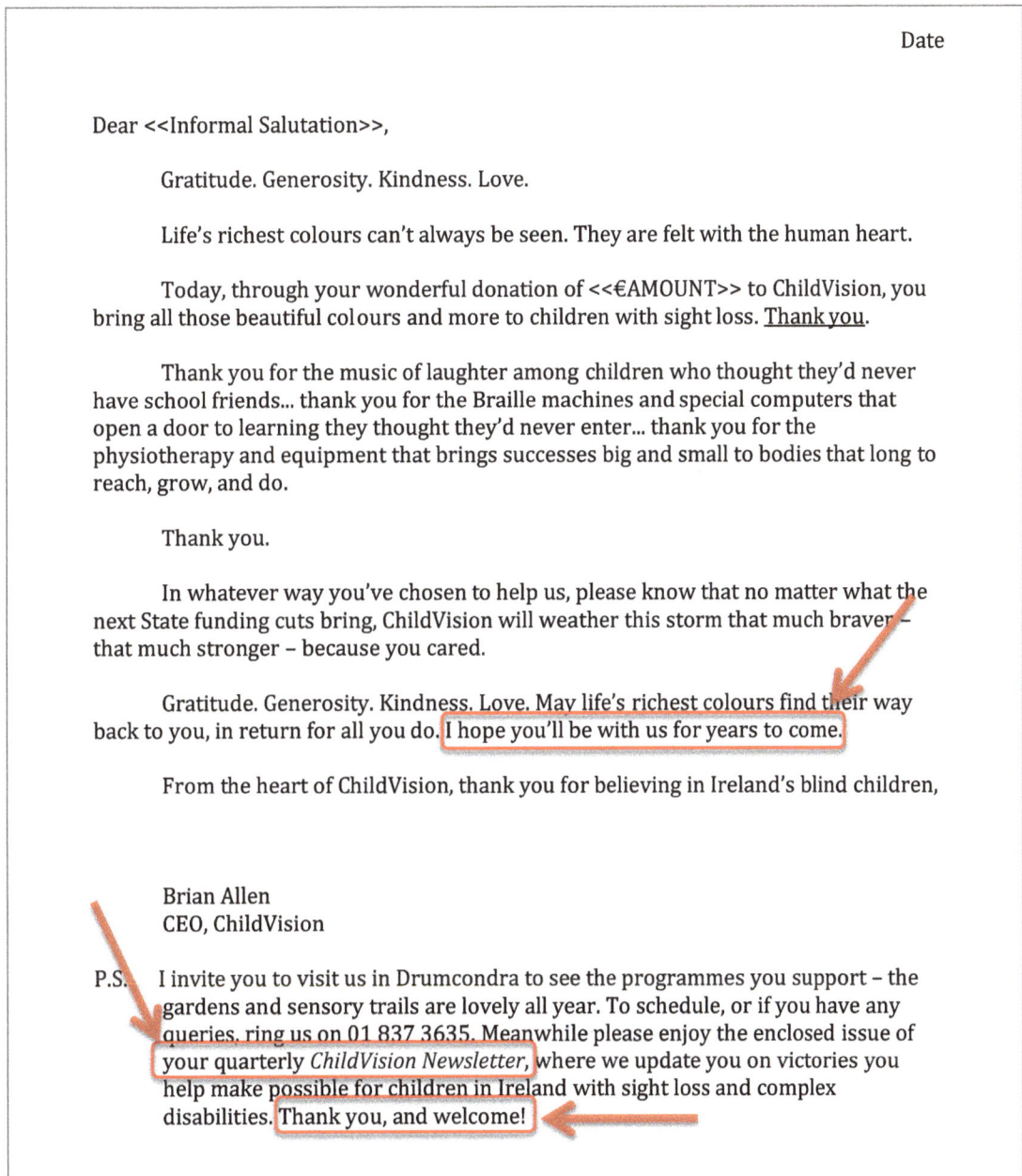

Date

Dear <<Informal Salutation>>,

Gratitude. Generosity. Kindness. Love.

Life's richest colours can't always be seen. They are felt with the human heart.

Today, through your wonderful donation of <<€AMOUNT>> to ChildVision, you bring all those beautiful colours and more to children with sight loss. Thank you.

Thank you for the music of laughter among children who thought they'd never have school friends... thank you for the Braille machines and special computers that open a door to learning they thought they'd never enter... thank you for the physiotherapy and equipment that brings successes big and small to bodies that long to reach, grow, and do.

Thank you.

In whatever way you've chosen to help us, please know that no matter what the next State funding cuts bring, ChildVision will weather this storm that much braver – that much stronger – because you cared.

Gratitude. Generosity. Kindness. Love. May life's richest colours find their way back to you, in return for all you do. I hope you'll be with us for years to come.

From the heart of ChildVision, thank you for believing in Ireland's blind children,

Brian Allen
CEO, ChildVision

P.S.   I invite you to visit us in Drumcondra to see the programmes you support – the gardens and sensory trails are lovely all year. To schedule, or if you have any queries, ring us on 01 837 3635. Meanwhile please enjoy the enclosed issue of your quarterly *ChildVision Newsletter*, where we update you on victories you help make possible for children in Ireland with sight loss and complex disabilities. Thank you, and welcome!

Copywriter: Lisa Sargent | Client: ChildVision

You're nearly there with your new donor thanking. There's just one more important detail you may or may not need to acknowledge... the premium.

Which brings us to point number four.

4. **Your first-time donor thank-you letter, if you also included a premium as part of the appeal mailing, needs to call attention to that.**

Without debating the pros and cons of premiums as part of acquisition mailings, the fact is, lots of nonprofits use them to inspire new donors to give.

A wildlife protection organization, for example, might include a tiger key fob in its mailing. Or address labels. We've created packs that have used ornaments, wrapping paper, note cards, and even tote bags. The point here is, *if* you included a premium, you need to say something about it to trigger the reader's memory – to connect it to the original donation and the good feelings around it.

Here's an example of a very simple paragraph that was inserted into the new donor thank-you letter to acknowledge a tote bag that was included in the acquisition mailing:

> I hope, too, that you are pleased with your ABC Charity tote bag, and I thank you for using it to spread the word about the lifesaving work of ABC.

It can truly be as simple as that!

You now have the essential tools to compose your new donor thank-you letters. But there's something else you can do <u>first</u>, that's practically magic...

In addition to sending a thank-you letter to first-time donors, you can call these special people to thank them. As you'll discover in Chapter 9, thank-you calls are magic for more than just first-time donors.

**They work wonders for everyone.
But first, the second-time donation thank you...**

CHAPTER

6

The second-time donation thank-you letter (Gratitude for faithful friends who often get overlooked)

"If you have the words,
there's always a chance
that you'll find the way."

— **Seamus Heaney,** *Irish poet, playwright, and Nobel Laureate*

You might be wondering why a second donation to your nonprofit warrants a special thank-you.

Well.

Short of a bequest, the Second Gift is an occasion that tops just about all other occasions in the life of a donor – and should be acknowledged as such. In other words, it's one of those hidden donor moments we discussed. And a powerful one, to boot.

How momentous of an occasion is the Second Gift, really?

The average retention rate of a first-time donor, as you know, hovers around twenty percent. This rate is so dismal that many fundraising experts don't consider these still-fickle friends as donors. They may simply be "impulse givers."

This isn't to diminish the grace and generosity behind a first donation. But rather, to reinforce that a second gift isn't a sure thing.

Once you've proven to your new donor that your organization is worthy of their continued generosity and they move from impulse giver to make that second donation…

Their retention rate increases to 60%[15].

Sixty percent, thankologists! Isn't that amazing? And more good news:

Your second-gift thank-you doesn't have to be fancy.
Just be genuine and warm, and acknowledge what you know.

To show you how simple a second-gift thank-you letter can be, here's an excerpt from an oldie but goody second-gift TY I wrote years ago:

Dear <<Salutation>>,

Here at MQI, we were incredibly grateful to receive your first gift.

Then to receive a second donation from you of €AMOUNT so people who are homeless and hungry in Ireland can continue to turn to Merchants Quay for help and hope – your generosity reaches far beyond words.

Thank you.

Just as your first donation did, the kindness of your second gift will be felt in the hot meals, one to

---

15 "The State of Donor Retention In One Image," Bloomerang. https://bloomerang.co/blog/the-state-of-donor-retention-in-one-image/

one counselling, basic medical care, recovery from addiction and so much more that MQI are now able to provide thanks to you.

But deeper than that, I wish you could see what your ongoing support means to the women and men who come through our doors. The relief on their faces as they realise that here, they are safe. Here, they are not invisible. Here, their lives can change.

Here, because of you.

This letter then goes on to tick off more essential building blocks that you now know... the PS, the invitation, the inclusion of a phone number donors can use if they have questions... and the like.

Also, all of these are hand-signed by the CEO.

At time of this writing, retention at MQI hovered around seventy percent. (Yes, 70%. That's <u>with</u> an active acquisition program too – so in other words, not a stagnating file.) Sweet? You bet.

But when it comes to truly spectacular donor retention rates, there's one group of supporters who pretty much have <u>everyone</u> beat.

You and I will explore how to thank these miracle-makers, next.

I can't get over how thankful you are for the little I send.

— T., a real-life donor who sent back a thank you on her 86th birthday

CHAPTER

CHAPTER

7

The monthly donation thank-you letter
(More gratitude for oft-overlooked faithful friends)

> "The single biggest problem in communication is the illusion that it has taken place."
>
> — **George Bernard Shaw**

A retention rate of sixty percent for second-time donors is noteworthy. But retention rates for monthly supporters are <u>stratospheric</u> by comparison.

The experts at Bloomerang report that the average retention rate of monthly givers, also called sustainers, is an eyebrow-raising 90%[16].

Nine out of ten of these giving hearts stay with you for the long haul!

---

16 "The State of Donor Retention In One Image," Bloomerang. https://bloomerang.co/blog/the-state-of-donor-retention-in-one-image/

The secret is because it's automatic – sustaining supporters give you permission to charge their credit card or directly debit their bank account with a set amount that they donate monthly (or sometimes quarterly).[17]

Even if you base your decision to thank solely on the massive lifetime value these steadfast supporters hold for your organization, that kind of commitment deserves to be recognized and lauded.

Which is exactly what you and I will explore now.

Gratitude for sustainers:
How you can do a better job of thanking
your monthly donors

The rules for sustainers are common sense.

At heart it comes down to thinking deeply about, and warmly acknowledging, the details around their monthly pledge of support.

In the paragraphs below, you'll find some examples of the different scenarios in which a monthly commitment comes to you, and ways you can thank a sustainer.

1.) <u>First-Time Monthly Gift</u>: Thanking a new donor who pledges their monthly support instead of single cash gift

If the first gift is a monthly pledge, that is, an individual becomes a monthly donor as part of an appeal and hasn't given before, your first-time thank-you letter needs to acknowledge this.

---

17 To learn more about how to start a monthly giving program, begin with the best: the stellar experts Erica Waasdorp, author of *Monthly Giving: The Sleeping Giant* and *Monthly Giving Made Easy,* and Harvey McKinnon, author of *How to Create Lifelong Donors Through Monthly Giving* and *Hidden Gold,* among others.

The sample below was sent on the inside of a notecard, short and sweet. In this case it was sent to new monthly donors to a regional hospital foundation's program called Healing Hands:

<<Handwritten Salutation>>,

Healing Hands needed you ... and you were there. Thank you.

Your kind pledge to support the Patient and Family Assistance Fund with a recurring monthly donation of <<$AMOUNT>> to ███████████ ████████ Healing Hands program has been gratefully received.

Please watch your mail for your Healing Hands welcome letter and official pledge details, arriving soon.

With my gratitude and warmest wishes,
<<Signature>>

The letter was hand-signed, had a warm closing, and was followed immediately by all the required details confirming the pledge and welcoming the supporter, in another heartfelt letter.

2.) <u>Upgrade to Monthly Gift</u>: Thanking a donor who previously gave one-time cash or credit card donations and has now chosen to donate monthly

If your donor has been a one-time cash/credit supporter and has just converted to a monthly supporter, or if they have chosen to increase the amount of their existing monthly gift, you need to acknowledge this.

In a thank-you letter, or in a thank-you card like the Healing Hands example, acknowledging the change in relationship can be as simple as the following:

I'm thrilled to learn you have strengthened your sustaining support for [Name of Nonprofit] to [$Amount] monthly. Thank you!

Or:

> Thank you so very much for being a dedicated partner to [Name of Nonprofit] and for your decision to become a subscriber through your recent pledge of [$Amount] monthly. This work is stronger because of you.

3.) <u>**Special Cash Gift From A Monthly Donor**</u>**: Thanking an individual who is already a monthly donor and who gives a special cash donation**

You may have heard the sad stories of donors becoming monthly supporters, then suddenly receiving no further appeal letters at all, ever.

<u>In my experience this is a mistake.</u>

We've found over the years that many monthly donors are happy and willing to make an "extra" donation in response to an appeal that inspires them. Especially during the holidays. Why deny them of that opportunity?

You can acknowledge their special generosity this way:

> As a steadfast monthly supporter of [Name of Nonprofit], you are already one of our most dedicated defenders of [Earth's last wild places, homeless animals, etc]. Now to receive your special donation this [spring, holiday, Giving Tuesday, in response to XXXX], it's hard to find the words to thank you enough. You are, truly, our heart and soul!

Next up: donations you receive in memory of someone's passing... "in lieu of flowers"...

CHAPTER

8

In lieu of flowers:
The memorial donation
thank-you letter[18]

"The life of the dead is placed in the
memory of the living."

— Marcus Tullius Cicero

The year after my mother broke our hearts and passed away after a fierce battle with metastatic breast cancer, I received a card from the hospice where Mom spent her final hours.

The card read:

*'Thinking of you and remembering your loved one
on the anniversary of your loss.'*

There was even a handwritten message.

---

18 A version of this chapter first made its debut as an article I wrote for SOFII, the Showcase of Fundraising Innovation and Inspiration, on May 21, 2012, https://sofii.org/article/in-lieu-of-flowers-how-to-write-lively-memorial-donation-thank-you-letters. Eternal gratitude to fundraising legend, and now my friend, Ken Burnett, for graciously giving my Thank-you Clinics a forever home there.

I was delighted and honored...

... Right up to the moment when my soul was CRUSHED.

The people who eased my mother's pain as she literally drew her last living breath, the place we entrusted with this resplendent gem of a human being's journey out of life, had spelled her name wrong.

In the handwritten message.

Her name was not just a little wrong, either. It was Other Galaxy Wrong.

Oh, the correct letters were all there. But they had been reassembled.

You see, like Elton John, George Michael, and Bea Arthur, my mom was one of those who had a first name that could also have been her last name.

In the card, Mom's first name was swapped with her last, which unofficially changed her gender (like if the late actress Bea Arthur was instead Arthur Bea).

THEN her middle initial was mysteriously tacked on at the very end of her first name, to form her "new" last name.

Heavy, woeful, heartbroken sigh. Didn't they know this was Mom?!

Mom!

I thought of sending a tribute gift, but I didn't. *I couldn't.* My trust was swept away in a single, shaky, tear-stained moment.

Getting memorial thank-yous wrong can shut down someone's future donations... forever.

With memorial donation thank-you letters – also called *in-memoriam thank-yous* – there are three main challenges.

We'll discuss each of these in turn.

Challenge 1: Death is a delicate subject.

The subject of death is especially delicate for you, the writer.

That's because most of you will have no idea what prompted the memorial donation in the first place.

Was it sent 'in lieu of flowers,' possibly from someone who didn't know the deceased all that well and maybe felt obligated? Or perhaps it was from a lifelong friend – or a grieving adult child – who is heartbroken beyond measure.

The point is, usually you just don't know... and you may never know.

All too often, the default response is to send an in-memoriam donation thank-you that's generic as cardboard.

Solution 1: Don't wallow in propriety.

Instead, remember what it is we all want.

<u>To know that others still think of us and that we have made a difference in this world.</u>

Picture those elements that <u>really</u> connect with human beings. Altruism. Immortality. Joy. Recognition. Compassion. Love.

Then <u>use these words</u> as inspiration for the beginning of your letter.

Here's an example of the lead sentences I wrote for an animal welfare charity's letter:

> In remembering someone who was dear to you, you also took the time to think of homeless pets.
>
> Thank you so much for your heartfelt gift of [Amount] to [Name of Charity] in memory of [Name of Deceased].

"Hold it right there," you cry. "That copy quite clearly says someone who was <u>dear</u> to you. Look, Lisa, I have no idea if they're dear or not!"

Good catch! Let's revise it slightly...

> In so kindly remembering the life of another, you also took the time to think of [the environment, people who are homeless, first generation college students, etc.].
>
> Thank you so much for your heartfelt gift of [Amount] to [Name of Charity] in memory of [Name of Deceased].

Or ...

> At a time when you were remembering another, you also took the time to think of [the environment, people who are homeless, first generation college students, etc.].
>
> Thank you so very much for your heartfelt gift of [Amount] to [Name of Charity] in memory of [Name of Deceased].

See how easy that was?

Here is yet another way to phrase your thank-you:

> Not long ago you generously thought of someone special… and [the environment, stray kittens, people who are homeless, etc.] too. Thank you for your kind gift of [Amount] to ABC charity, in memory of [Name of Deceased].

And one more:

> Because of you, the memory of [Name of Deceased] will live on in the smile of each child helped here at [Name of Charity]. Thank you for your heartfelt donation of [Amount], which we received on [Date].

But there are still a few pieces missing. Let's look at those next.

Challenge 2: Most memorial and tribute donations require not one, but <u>TWO</u> letters... with the correct details in each.

If you aren't sending <u>two letters</u> as part of a memorial donation, in most cases, you're only doing half the job.

Allow me to illustrate.

<u>Case in point</u>: Roy makes a memorial gift in honor of his coworker Stan's mother, who passed away recently.

You need a thank-you to Roy <u>and</u> a separate letter to Stan.

But how do you handle the copy for each?

Solution 2: Apply some common sense.

I say common sense here, but when it comes to memorial donation thank-yous, the truth is closer to the old saw "common sense isn't common."

You'd be shocked at the number of memorial thank-you letters I see where the *recipient*, or in our case Stan, is being thanked for a donation they didn't make.

Or where the donor, in this case Roy, is never told that Stan was notified of Roy's gift.

These errors will not only tarnish the character of your nonprofit, they will also mar the precious memory of someone's beloved.

Knowing this, let's turn our attention back to Roy and Stan, and think through the donation. Because while it's not complicated, it <u>is</u> vital...

Roy made the gift.

Stan did not; it's his mother (RIP) being honored.

So for Roy, the key points here are:

- 💜 Roy gets thanked and the confirmation that his gift was received
- 💜 Roy is reassured you are honoring the correct person (Stan's mom)
- 💜 Roy is <u>also</u> reassured the correct person (Stan) will be notified of his donation.

How do you write it? Like this:

> At a time when you were remembering another, you also took the time to think of [the environment, people who are homeless, first generation college students, etc.].
>
> Thank you so very much for your heartfelt gift of [Amount] to [Name of Charity] in memory of [Name of Deceased]. At the time of your thoughtful donation, you also let us know you'd like [Name of Person Being Notified, in this case, Stan] to be notified of your kind memorial donation, and we'd like you to know that a lovely remembrance notecard is on its way.

In Roy's thank-you letter, you will also call on the building blocks and essentials you learned in earlier chapters, including, for example, letting him know when he'll next hear from you (such as in your donor newsletter), and how he can reach you with questions.

But what kind of letter should Stan receive?

The key points of his letter are different than Roy's, of course. But you'll be happy to know you can modify much of Roy's letter.

For Stan's letter, the key points are two:

- 💜 Stan gets a warm and kind notification that Roy made a thoughtful gift to honor the passing of Stan's mother
- 💜 Stan does <u>not</u> get thanked for donating, because he didn't.

So here's how you modify the letter to Stan:

> Someone kindly took the time to think of you today… and [the environment, stray kittens, people who are homeless, etc.] too. [Name of Person Who Made The Gift] made a thoughtful donation from the heart to ABC charity, in memory of [Name of Deceased].

I'll say it one more time.

As it should be with everything you write to the donors and friends of your nonprofit, the overarching wisdom for these previous paragraphs is simple.

<u>Before</u> you put pen to paper or fingers to keyboard, think through the gift you've received and ask these questions:

- ♥ Who needs to be thanked?
- ♥ Who needs to be notified?
- ♥ Is the information I have on file correct?
- ♥ Does the information in the database make sense?
- ♥ Is there a meaningful way to connect with them in the future, and what might need to be revised to acknowledge their connection to our cause?

Which brings us to the third and final challenge of memorial thank-you letters…

Challenge 3: Memorial and tribute donor stewardship beyond the first gift and thank-you.

Memorial gifts are one and done, right?

After all, you only die once.

And what of the memorial gift's close cousin, the tribute donation?

Those gifts people make to commemorate a special occasion for a person or people who are still living, like a wedding, for example.

Isn't that single, special memorial or tribute gift the end of it all? Well, it doesn't have to be...

From where I stand, the problem with keeping memorial donors connected and giving is more due to the way organizations have historically approached these donors. Not the result of any unwillingness on the part of the donor.

Why do I say this?

Because after the memorial or tribute thank-you, these compassionate donors – who really did think of a bigger cause to honor someone's passing – are often treated to silence.

A donor communications vacuum. The badlands of loyalty.

So if most nonprofits never communicate with memorial donors again, how can we have the foggiest notion of whether a lack of repeat gifts is due to unwillingness on their part?

There are plenty of timely and relevant ways to be in touch with both donors and families of the deceased after a memorial gift is made.

Can you welcome these new friends, even in their sorrow? Yes.

Can you make it heartwarming for them? Yes.

Can you start today? Yes.

Solution 3: Try these...

The post-memorial donation cover letter:

Let's return for a moment to our memorial donation example from the beginning of this chapter, with the story of Stan and Roy.

You'll recall that Stan and Roy are coworkers. Stan's mom passed away, and Roy made a memorial donation to your organization. Let's assume you rightly, warmly, and appropriately wrote back to both Stan and Roy.

It doesn't have to end there.

To your new supporter welcome packet, or to your regular donor newsletter, why not include a thoughtful cover letter reflecting the fact that you know this is the result of a memorial donation?

Here's how the first paragraph of your cover letter might look for Stan:

> I thought you'd like to know about some of the wonderful things that have come about for [the environment, stray kittens, people who are homeless, e.g.] in memory of YYYY, who will forever be remembered as a result of XXX's recent and incredibly kind gift.

And the same lead paragraph adapted for Roy:

> I thought you'd like to know about some of the wonderful things that have come about for [the environment, stray kittens, people who are homeless, e.g..] since your recent gift made in memory of YYYY, who will forever be remembered as a result of your kindness and generosity.

Wouldn't this help both Stan and Roy to feel seen, and help Stan to know that the memory of someone he cared about was living on?

Of course it would – and it's a warm glow that, if done properly and as the next section illustrates, can be repeated a year later.

The anniversary note:

Remember what we <u>all</u> want when we die: to have made a difference.

This means, <u>at a bare minimum</u>, you can send an anniversary note to honor the one-year anniversary of the last gift. (Remember those donor moments we talked about at the start of Part II on page 52? This is a perfect example.)

And to continue our example, it can be easily modified to address both Stan and Roy.

<u>To Stan our beautiful card can read</u>: *'On the anniversary of your loss'*

The card then goes on to add a quick word about how the memory of NAME lives on and what the gifts made in NAME's honor accomplished over the past year. You might even be able to close by mentioning a giving opportunity (tactfully, gently, softly), maybe an annual memorial. You could include a remittance envelope, postage-paid.

<u>To Roy</u>: *'Remembering your kindness one year later'*

This is a thank-you to Roy for his amazing act of kindness that, like Stan's, goes on to talk about the great things the gift accomplished in memory of another. And this could also close with a relevant giving opportunity — or even include a generic reply and postage-paid envelope for Roy, in case he would ever like to make another donation in memory of, or in tribute to, someone else.

I realize all of this thinking around a single donation may feel overwhelming. But imagine if the loved one who passed was yours. Or if you were the one who made that heartfelt gift to honor a dear friend in their hour of grief.

Now imagine how wonderful it would feel to you if all the details were accurate, and the letter arrived promptly, carrying a warm and genuine message.

That's the feeling you want to capture.

A final nice-to-have for further consideration:
The memorial donation summary letter to family/relatives

If the person who's passed away, or their surviving loved one, has requested donations be made to your organization in lieu of flowers, you may find yourself receiving multiple memorial donations. Wouldn't it be thoughtful for loved ones who are grieving, then, to send them a periodic summary of the kind gifts you've received – so they can personally contact people who've given if they choose?

Of course it would. And it can be this simple:

> Please accept our heartfelt sympathy at the loss of your [husband and father, life partner and friend, etc.]. We are deeply honored to receive donations in [Name's] memory, and promise to carry on the work in their name.
>
> All of us at [Name of Organization] are holding you in our thoughts, and wanted to be sure you know of the generous hearts doing the same, who have made donations to date in [Name's] memory:
>
> | | |
> |---|---|
> | Jane Doe | 789 Alpha Street, Anytown, ST 12345 |
> | Pete Álvarez and Kevin Smith | 88 Beta Avenue, Nextcity, ST 56789 |
> | Michelle Washington, MD | 444 Delta Circle, Thirdplace, ST 65432 |
>
> We've sent messages of thanks to each of the kind people listed above, and will of course continue to do so as gifts come in. We'll also update you on future donations, should you want to reach out personally to those who've given.
>
> If you have any questions, I'm just a phone call or email away on [phone number] or [email] and would be happy to help you.

Then continue with your closing and signature.

One last, loving detail. If the person who passed was a supporter of your organization, it would be so thoughtful for the family to know the good that supporter did in their lifetime – even if your special card or note describes their kindness in broad strokes, their generosity made your work and the world better, and letting the family know would be a generous tribute all your own. ♥

PART III:

Thanking is not just for donations: more places to drip-feed supporter gratitude for even bigger results and retention

---

"Appreciation can make a day - even change a life. Your willingness to put it into words is all that is necessary."

— Margaret Cousins

---

you are amazing ☺

Imagine every day you take the exact same route to work. Same turns. Same scene. Same stops...

One day, the view from the train or your car or your bicycle changes.

A sign appears by the side of the roadway, attached to a plain wooden post. Bright blue letters populate the simple white sign in less than perfect handwriting.

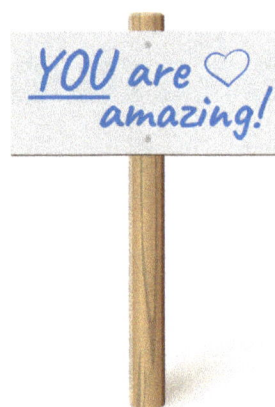

The sign reads:
Thank you for the incredible work
you do. <u>YOU</u> are amazing!

Okay, okay, you tell yourself. It's just a sign by the side of the road.

But you can't help it. That message gives your spirits a lift on an otherwise mundane day.

Somehow, you feel better about yourself. Better about your job.

Better even about the fact that there was no creamer for your coffee when you went to the break room.

Thank you for the incredible work you do. <u>YOU</u> are amazing!, that little sign echoes in your head.

So you smile, shrug your shoulders, and tell yourself you could do without all the extra calories of coffee creamer anyway.

The next day you look for the sign, but it's gone.

The day after that, too.

And you can't say why – after all it was just a sign – but you feel a pang of sadness and loss. Like a little light just went out of the world.

By the third or fourth or fifteenth day, you've all but forgotten it was ever there, and how you felt that day you saw it.

Do <u>not</u> let your donor thank-you letter be that little white sign. It cannot sustain the warm glow of giving... cannot survive... on its own.

I'm not exaggerating here.

And you do not need to write as many appeals and newsletters and emails and thank-yous as I do in a year – which is *a lot* – to know what I know:

People are longing for meaning in this world!

Longing for connection!

Longing to be part of something bigger.

Now, if your organization starts thanking donors the way I discuss in this book, you'll be a million steps closer to helping them feel connected. But those thank-yous can't be the only good thing a donor receives from you.

You need more than that single little signpost to lift them up.

Otherwise, they forget. <u>Or worse: they worry that *you* forgot</u>.

Plus... since they probably support more than one cause like the average donor does[19], don't you want to be the one to hold a special place in their heart?

Yes, oh yes, you do.

So let's look at how to kindle the warm glow of giving all year – because the world needs more goodness.

---

19 According to multiple sources, the average American supports 4.5 charities. Agree or don't, suffice to say that they probably donate to more than your nonprofit alone.

CHAPTER

CHAPTER

9

I just called to say "We Love You!":
The magic of donor thank-you phone calls

"... I had found a joy I never expected as I thought about clearing my desk. It wasn't the joy of finishing the job, or getting through the pile. It wasn't even the joy of remembering why we do the work we do.

It was the joyful sound a 'thank you' makes when it lands in a donor's heart."

— **Hildy Gottlieb,** *The Sound A Thank You Makes* [20]

---

20 Because everyone in fundraising should read this article in full: "The Sound a Thank You Makes," by Hildy Gottleib. Huffington Post, December 9, 2014. https://www.huffpost.com/entry/the-sound-a-thank-you-makes_b_6291448

The incredible author and social change theorist Hildy Gottlieb delivers one of the most beautiful first-hand accounts on the power of thank-you calls that I've ever read.

Her story isn't about numbers or retention or results.

It's about, as she puts it so eloquently, "the joyful sound a 'thank you' makes when it lands in a donor's heart."

For our purposes in this chapter, thank-you calls are about how you can duplicate the heartfelt magic Hildy describes, <u>and</u> what happens after you do.

<u>Because what happens *after* a thank-you call holds a magic all its own.</u>

If you were to call and thank your first-time donors within 48 hours of receiving their gift, here's what can happen.

The body of research and testing conducted by Penelope Burk shows that thank-you calls to donors from board members made within 24 to 48 hours of receiving the donation increased the amount of the donor's next gift by 39% over those who didn't receive a call. (The callers, it should be noted, did <u>not</u> ask for another gift.)

<u>After 14 months, these donors were still giving 42% more than the non-called group</u>.

As jaw-dropping, four percent of the donors in the TY call test group expressed an interest in "doing something more."[21]

Think about that for a moment, just in terms of the power to help increase a person's second gift by an average of thirty-nine percent alone.

That's the difference between receiving a donation of $50 and a donation of almost $70, from people who – according to Burk's testing – were still giving more than the non-called group over a year later.

---

21 *Donor-Centered Fundraising*, Penelope Burk, page 57, 2018, https://cygresearch.com/product/donor-centered-fundraising-new-edition/.

Now if you've been around the sector awhile, you may know that the first version of Burk's book, *Thanks! A Guide to Donor-Centred Fundraising*, was published in the UK, in November 2000 – and in the US, in June 2003.[22]

I can practically hear the hard eyerolls at this. *"That's soooo outdated, Lisa. Donors today would never behave this way!"* some of you might be thinking.

The truth is, it's not outdated. Not by a long shot.

In fact, as revealed by Bloomerang's massive 2020 analysis of donor second-gift habits, thank-you calls still have a quantifiable and significantly positive effect on giving and retention...

In a comprehensive analysis of its extensive customer base encompassing 3,729 nonprofits in Canada and the United States (that included the giving habits of more than 1.95 *million* donors between 2012 and 2018), Bloomerang found that new donors who received a thank-you call within the first 90 days of making their gift were retained 41.24% of the time.

Without the call? 33.01%.

Want more?

The research also found that phone calls increased the average amount of the second gift... by double.

Yes, double: from $50 to $100.

The calls also – *get ready for it* – cut the elapsed time to the second donation from 261 days in the no-call group, to 217 days in the one-call group. (Unsure why this matters? We'll unpack the importance of second-gift timing in just a few more moments.)

There was a multiple-call cohort, by the way. More than one thank-you phone call to these givers prompted a second gift just 53 days after the first

---

22 Penelope Burk, *Donor-Centered Fundraising* (Chicago: Cygnus Applied Research, 2003).

one, which means those multiple calls almost certainly happened sometime in the first six weeks after the original donation.[23]

Still need more? Here's another analysis of more than six thousand donors...

CDR Fundraising Group unearthed equally enlightening data around the positive effect of thank-you calls.

A test conducted by CDR Fundraising Group, a direct response fundraising firm headquartered in Maryland, involved 6,225 one- or multiple-time donors who in the previous year had given between $50 and $249.99 to a disaster appeal.

<u>They found that thank-you calls increased the subsequent gift *rate* by as much as forty-seven percent</u>!

The thank-you calls also increased the average *gift* by 8.3% over the group that received no call.[24]

See what I mean by magic?

Just by looking back to those four pieces of research and results, you can glean some valuable insights about how to do effective thank-you calls.

In particular, these essential takeaways:

- 💜 **Make new donor thank-you calls promptly.** In Burk's research, new donors were called within 48 hours of receiving their gift.
- 💜 **Make thank-you calls from board members if at all possible.** Also effective are staff and vested, grateful, longtime volunteers.
- 💜 **Do NOT ask for another donation** in the call.
- 💜 **Consider testing multiple calls to new donors.** Remember, Bloomerang's analysis of multi-call recipients cut the speed to second gift by more than 150 days.

---

23 "Actually, Calling Donors To Thank Them Does Make Them More Likely To Give Again (and Give More)," Heidi Atkinson, Bloomerang, March 2020, https://bloomerang.co/blog/actually-calling-donors-to-thank-them-does-make-them-more-likely-to-give-again-and-give-more/.

24 "Test Shows Reaction of 6,225 Donors," NonProfit Times, https://www.thenonprofittimes.com/npt_articles/test-shows-reaction-6225-donors/.

Below you'll find an example of a basic first-time donor thank-you call script to build from[25]:

```
        Hi, this is _____ calling. I'm [on
the all-volunteer Board of Directors at name of
organization], and staff there told me you recently
made your first donation. I wanted to call you
personally to say a big thank you, and welcome.
Your generosity means so much to this work we do,
and I just wanted you to know. Thanks for helping
make a difference in [organization's mission, for
example, "in the fight to end animal abuse"]. Have
a great [day/evening], and thank you so much again!
```

It would be absolutely <u>brilliant</u> if you could call and thank everyone, regardless of the gift's size. But depending on your organization and the number of passionate, willing people you have available to make the calls, you probably won't be able to. In which case, single out new donors, people who've given for a long time, monthly supporters (even once a year is fine), major givers, mid-level supporters, and those who've recently increased their gift – meaning, it's not all about the size of the gift. Loyalty and connection matter too.

Let's adapt our first-time donor thank-you call script for an existing supporter:

```
        Hi, this is _____ calling. I'm [on
the all-volunteer Board of Directors at name
of organization], and staff there told me you
recently made another donation. I wanted to
call you personally to say a big thank you! Your
generosity means so much to this work we do, and
I just wanted you to know. Thanks for helping
make a difference in [organization's mission, for
example, "in the fight to end animal abuse"]. Have
a great[day/evening], and thank you so much again!
```

---

25 First-time donor thank-you call script adapted from, and with the full permission and blessing of, fundraising coach, leadership expert, author, and speaker extraordinaire, Marc A. Pitman of The Concord Leadership Group. More sound advice on thank-you calls from the always fabulous Marc, here: https://fundraisingcoach.com/thank-you-script/

Of course, your callers won't connect with a person one hundred percent of the time. This means you also want a brief, simple variation of the script that allows you to leave an appreciative message and a number where you can be reached should your supporter want to call back. As simple as:

> ```
> If you ever have any questions, please give us
> a call at _____. Our [donor care coordinator]
> is [Name], and she'd be delighted to help you.
> Thank you again!
> ```

The bottom line is, keep it short and sweet.
AND...

.... In your tip sheet for callers, remind them to be relaxed and open, and – *even though the message they share is short* – not to rush it.

I say all this because my clients who make these first-time donor calls frequently report that supporters are delighted by the fact that you aren't asking for a donation and don't intend to.

With the pressure off, they're often eager to have a chat with your caller about the work or their gift, and even to share their personal giving story. Don't let this moment slip away in a rush to reach the end of the script!

Instead, coach your team in advance – and if you can, in your thank-you call script and tip sheet, include a "next step" bullet point with a sample follow-up question or two.

For example, after the initial thank-you call script, you might add a few open-ended questions – something simple like the following:

♥ If the supporter seems eager to talk, ask a follow-up question like, "If you're comfortable sharing your story, what inspired you to become a supporter?"

It also pays to have a think in advance about other questions your supporters might ask about the work, and arm your callers with a list of resources, contact names and numbers, and talking points to answer those questions. Questions about events and tours, for example – or legacy gifts.

As the saying goes, the harder you work, the luckier you get.

Last but not least, earlier in this chapter I promised we'd unpack the importance of second gift timing – and why it's so massive that thank you phone calls can decrease the time to second gift:

For this we turn to Bill Jacobs over at The Analytical Ones, who delivered a mic drop moment with the below graph showing the 5-year value of a donor based on how quickly an organization inspires a new donor to make a second gift.

In Jacobs' own words, "the correlation is astounding":

Source: The Analytical Ones [online]. "The Exponential Importance of Second Gift Timing," Bill Jacobs. https://www.analyticalones.com/the-exponential-importance-of-second-gift-timing/
Also featured in iDonate's 2021 free ebook, Donor Retention & the Connected Giving Org, https://word.nten.org/wp-content/uploads/2021/03/CG_eBook.pdf.

Your organization's data might be slightly different than this graph, it's true. But odds are good that if you can inspire a second gift within the first six months as opposed to 7-12 months, you'll still be looking at a jump in the five-year value of your new donors.

One of the best ways to do that? Begin by thanking your new donors promptly and well for the first gift... including a thank-you phone call or two.

Now let's look at another powerful place to drip-feed gratitude... your donor newsletter.

CHAPTER
10

The grateful newsletter:
What even really good donor newsletters are still missing

"Excellence, quality, and good should be earned words, attributed by others to us, not proclaimed by us about ourselves."

— **Ed Catmull**, *Creativity, Inc.*

There is a donor who saves every newsletter a nonprofit sends.

In fact, Rose loves those newsletters so much she keeps them in a shoebox. She returns to them like old friends, to lift her spirits from time to time.

Rose is not her real name. Her story, though, is true. And yes, it is an actual shoebox. I know because she wrote to tell my client so.

For every euro this organization invests in producing and printing Rose's beloved donor newsletter, supporters give back SIX more in donations. (You read that return on investment right: it's a 6:1 ROI. Sometimes, it's seven times more.)

**I think of Rose every time I write a newsletter.
I ask myself, "Is it shoebox-worthy?"
If not, I work harder.**

And one of the things that does not, <u>and will never</u>, make your newsletter shoebox-worthy is if you fill it with stories of how great <u>you</u> are as an organization... or how you just got a giant check from some foundation (including photo of same)... or how your gala just raised a gazillion dollars and fifteen celebrities attended.

Great, effective, and powerful supporter newsletters are all about what your <u>*donors*</u> make possible. What <u>*they*</u> do, by giving. The lives <u>*they*</u> touch. The wrongs they right.

It's about how those good things couldn't happen without them.

**If you want to keep doing the work you do,
your donor newsletter must be about your donor.**

How to do proper donor newsletters is a topic unto itself, and experts like Tom Ahern[26] and Steven Screen[27] have gone a long way towards showing us the way (as has the amazing Jeff Brooks, who years ago helped create and refine what is now called The Domain Formula for donor newsletters).

But for this chapter, we will limit our focus to expressing gratitude.

Just as with thank-you letters, your goal with thanking in donor newsletters is to lift your language above the ordinary. Let's explore a few grateful newsletter tips and real-world examples to get you started:

---

26 *Making Money With Donor Newsletters,* by Tom Ahern, published by Emerson & Church, https://hilborn-civilsectorpress.com/products/making-money-with-donor-newsletters-ebook.

27 "10 Steps to Create a Money-Raising, Donor-Delighting Print Newsletter," The Better Fundraising Co. [online] https://betterfundraising.com/10-steps-ebook/. Free on sign-up.

1. **<u>Grateful Newsletter Tip #1:</u>** <u>Use your newsletter to report back and say thank you to donors on the topic of your last appeal</u>:

   One of the most important jobs – if not THE most important job – of your supporter newsletter is to report back to donors on what their gifts made possible. This one is specific. A hospital foundation in Napa Valley thanked donors after they helped build a new women's imaging center for earlier cancer detection:

Adventist Health St. Helena's incredible new Women's Imaging Center opens October 28th!

100% Built By <u>You</u>: Bringing Napa Valley Women A Lifesaving New Image

<u>THE GOAL</u>: Build a comprehensive women's imaging center with the best technology and the best team in a rural Napa Valley community of less than 7,000. Equip it with everything women need for the earliest cancer detection, best bone density scanning, and much more.

<u>THE MISSION</u>? Accomplished! Learn about the new women's imaging center that's 100% built by you...

As this newsletter went to press, the last of the finishing touches were underway at the new Women's Imaging Center in preparation for the October 28th ribbon cutting celebration. And what a celebration it will be, because this is the place that you, quite literally, made real. Because of donations like yours to St. Helena Hospital Foundation, women will no longer have to travel out of the area for advanced breast imaging and bone density scanning – screening and diagnostic tests that are critical to both quality of life and the earliest possible cancer detection.

A glimpse at what your generosity is making real at the new women's imaging center...

- **3D mammography** – also called tomography or tomosynthesis, this remarkable technology lets your radiologist scroll through detailed, crystal-clear images of your breast tissue like the pages of a book, often detecting cancers missed by 2D mammography (see sidebar page 4). This is because the radiologist views four images in traditional 2D mammograms vs. <u>thirty-two</u> in new 3D mammograms. Eight times more!

- **DEXA bone density testing** – one out of every two women over the age of 50 will break a bone due to osteoporosis, and a bone density scanning is the only way to tell if you have it before a fall happens.

- **Breast fellowship-trained readers** – Breast fellowship-trained means your images are read by radiologists who elect to receive up to two additional years of training in reading breast images.

- **Certified breast nurse navigator** – through the National

Copywriter: Lisa Sargent | Design: Sandie Collette, S. Collette Design
Client: Glen Newhart, CFRE, President and CEO, St. Helena Hospital Foundation

2. <u>**Grateful Newsletter Tip #2:** Bring numbers to life in your newsletter for your analytical readers, and reinforce how their gift is working</u>:

Some readers, we know, are show-me-the-numbers types. For these supporters you can use a simple infographic to report back. And be sure to add a thank you!

BECAUSE OF YOU...

9,500

families across Ethiopia, Kenya, Honduras and Zimbabwe secured access to water last year because of your support. **Thank you for caring.** 💙

Recent Projects You've Helped Fund:
Healing Made Possible by You...

one
Precision, safety & comfort:
1 orthopedic spine surgery table

four
Lifesaving labor & delivery:
4 Fetal Monitors

one
Capturing the human heart in a single beat: 1 amazing 512-slice CT scanner (currently funding)

two
Increased patient safety:
2 NAD Apollo enhanced anesthesia systems

six
Baby bonding 24/7:
6 additional NICView Cameras to meet increased demand

new
Better heart care:
New cardiac ablation equipment

thank you!
And much, much more. Thank you for touching the lives of patients, close to home. **Thank you for supporting Tri-City Hospital Foundation.**

How are your donations working? Let us count the ways —

Thank You for a Thousand Warm Welcomes

A safe place to rest, when before there was cold, hard pavement. A caring voice, where once there was no one. A 'how are you feeling?' and a hot meal, when all the other doors were closed. In 2017 at MQI, just a single year, these were some of the wonders worked by kind support like yours...

25,341 lunches for women and men who would have gone hungry

172 young people aged 18 to 25, supported on a path out of homelessness

19,368 sleeping mats rolled out at the Night Café Emergency Shelter

1,668 people turned to MQI for the first time – over a thousand warm welcomes!

148 pairs of weary feet given care and relief through MQI chiropody

419 homeless women and men helped by MQI's mental health team

Copywriter: Lisa Sargent | Design: Sandie Collette, S. Collette Design
Clients: Trócaire (top left), and MQI (left bottom), Tri-City Hospital Foundation (right), donor newsletters

3. **Grateful Newsletter Tip #3:** Tuck thanks into your masthead

Why not turn a masthead (what I call the footer because we put it on the back page, almost always, and save the prime real estate up front for stories) into one last place to say thank you? That way when they close the newsletter, gratitude is what you leave them with.

The work of Fighting Blindness is 90% funded by you, our members. Thank you for your support!

Fighting Blindness

Copywriter: Lisa Sargent | Design: Sandie Collette, S. Collette Design
Client: Fighting Blindness

4. **Grateful Newsletter Tip #4:** Add gratitude to the end of your newsletter articles:

The stories aren't possible without your donors, because the work you do isn't possible without them. The end of an article is the perfect place to add a thank-you. Here's a look at a super-simple example:

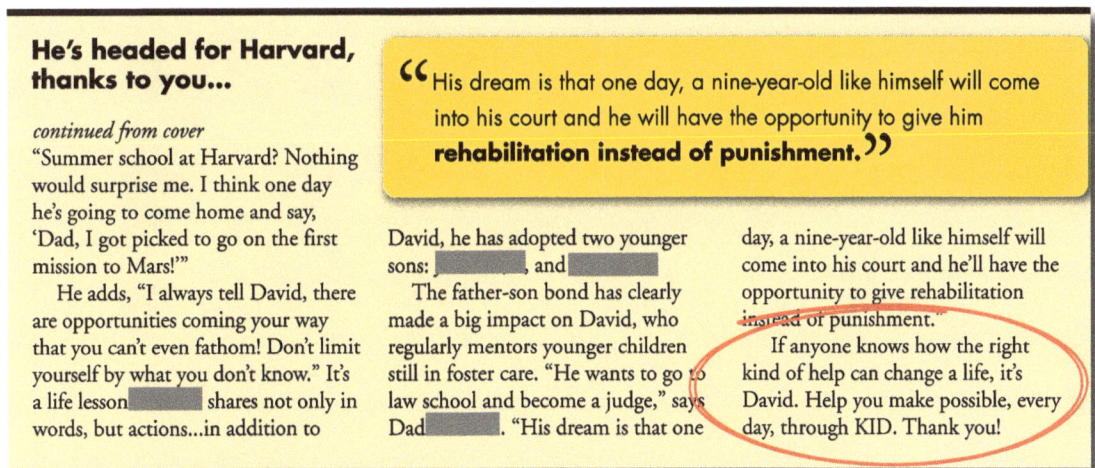

He's headed for Harvard, thanks to you...

continued from cover
"Summer school at Harvard? Nothing would surprise me. I think one day he's going to come home and say, 'Dad, I got picked to go on the first mission to Mars!'"

He adds, "I always tell David, there are opportunities coming your way that you can't even fathom! Don't limit yourself by what you don't know." It's a life lesson ████ shares not only in words, but actions...in addition to

"His dream is that one day, a nine-year-old like himself will come into his court and he will have the opportunity to give him **rehabilitation instead of punishment.**"

David, he has adopted two younger sons: ████, and ████

The father-son bond has clearly made a big impact on David, who regularly mentors younger children still in foster care. "He wants to go to law school and become a judge," says Dad ████. "His dream is that one

day, a nine-year-old like himself will come into his court and he'll have the opportunity to give rehabilitation instead of punishment."

If anyone knows how the right kind of help can change a life, it's David. Help you make possible, every day, through KID. Thank you!

Copywriter: Lisa Sargent | Design: Sandie Collette, S. Collette Design
Client: Kids In Distress

5. **Grateful Newsletter Tip #5:** Add thank-you to your headlines:

Full attribution and respect: Donor communications author and specialist Tom Ahern talked about this before I did. We just took his advice and ran with it, and now so can you. You can easily add a "Thank You" directly into your newsletter headline.

Here's how we did it for one client:

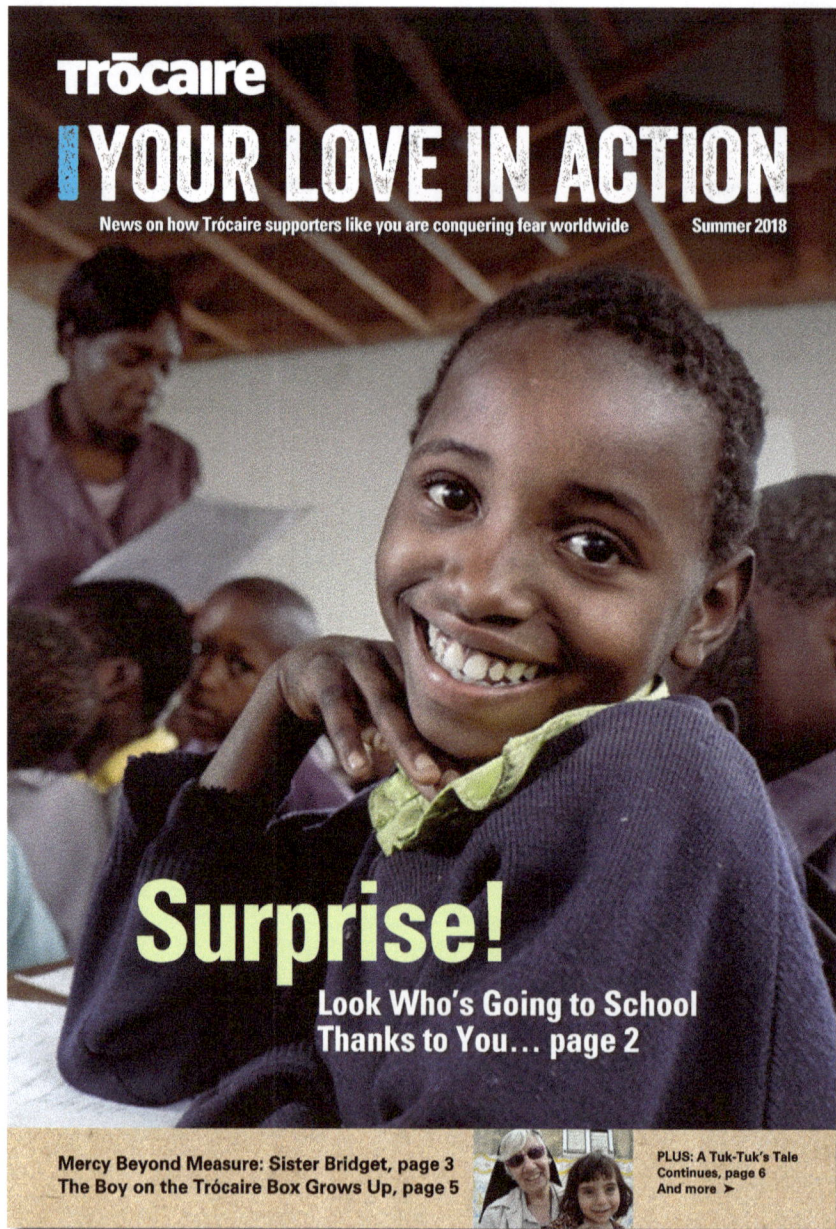

Copywriter: Lisa Sargent | Design: Sandie Collette, S. Collette Design
Client: Trócaire

6. **Grateful Newsletter Tip #6:** <u>Put the thanks on the envelope your newsletter is mailed in</u>: And yes, you need to send your newsletter in an envelope. Unless you're keen to have your response rate plummet by about half[28]).

Use an envelope, like this:

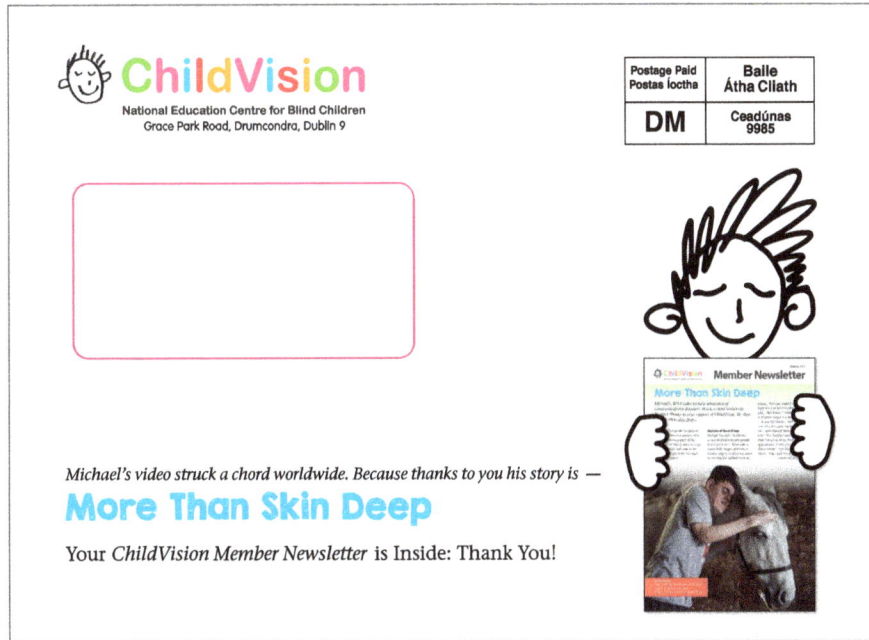

Copywriter: Lisa Sargent | Design: Sandie Collette, S. Collette Design
Client: ChildVision

Or this:

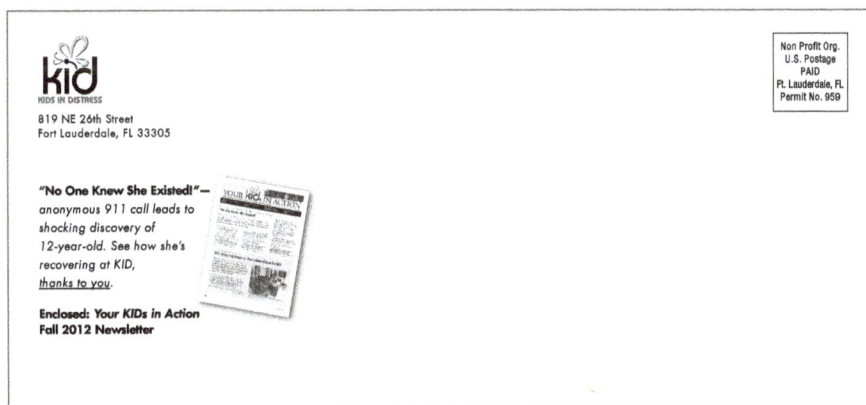

Copywriter: Lisa Sargent | Design: Sandie Collette, S. Collette Design
Client: Kids In Distress (KID)

---

28 "Keys to Creating a Failing Nonprofit Newsletter," Future Fundraising Now, Jeff Brooks. https://www.futurefundraisingnow.com/future-fundraising/2010/04/keys-to-creating-a-failing-nonprofit-newsletter.html

7. **Grateful Newsletter Tip #7:** <u>Instead of a president's letter on the inside of your newsletter, use a separate cover letter – and thank there, too.</u>

Here's an excerpt from the cover letter for an issue of St. Helena Hospital Foundation's supporter newsletter – note how it both thanks and introduces the newsletter that's also enclosed with the letter:

Adventist Health | **St. Helena Hospital Foundation**

10 Woodland Road
St. Helena, CA 94574
707.963.6208 Phone
shhfoundation@ah.org
www.shhfoundation.org
Tax ID # 20-1384250

<<Name>>
<<Addressee>>
<<Address Line 1>>
<<Address Line 2>>
<<City, State Zip>

President's Update – Fall 2021
From the Desk of Glen W. Newhart

Dear <<Salutation>>,

Stronger together, no matter what.

It's been said that when times are at their toughest, we discover our true strength – as a St. Helena Hospital Foundation family, as a community – by simply getting back up and doing the next, right thing, one day at a time.

Your enclosed Fall 2021 supporter newsletter tells that amazing story.

The story of how together, <u>as a direct result of your incredible philanthropic donations and your commitment to the best local healthcare</u>, we are stronger...

How in the middle of a pandemic, you continue helping build <u>the most advanced primary stroke care program in Napa County</u>...

How through every wave of Covid, your generosity is stocking Adventist Health St. Helena's free community vaccine clinics, with no government funding, and keeping our donor-funded Mobile Health Unit on the job nearly every day of the week...

Because you – *like all of us Adventist Health St. Helena* **– believe the <u>best</u> healthcare belongs not two hours away, but right here at home.**

And then you give, of your time, of your heart and soul, of your resources, to make that healthcare accessible and extraordinary for everyone.

<u>Thank you for giving</u>. <u>Thank you for caring</u>. Thank you for your ongoing vision to help build a hospital that is everything *this* community needs – whether

(read more, over)

Copywriter: Lisa Sargent | Design: Sandie Collette, S. Collette Design
Client: Glen Newhart, CFRE, President and CEO, St. Helena Hospital Foundation

8. **<u>Grateful Newsletter Tip #8:</u>** <u>Include a reply slip, and thank again</u>. (And if space allows, also include cut-and-send reply in your newsletter in case it's shared.)

Here's a cut-and-send sample, courtesy of KID:

Please help a child today.

Large or small, every gift you send to Kids In Distress will work wonders for children and families in need across South Florida. What can KID do? With help from you:

- **$25** can provide a boy or girl with a good pair of shoes (children often come to KID with nothing on their feet)
- **$50** covers the cost of an approved infant car seat, for a family who couldn't otherwise afford it
- **$75** is enough to pay for a young person's first dental exam at the KID Dental Clinic
- **$100** could supply a child with a crisp new school uniform – including shoes and socks!
- **$250** can provide a newborn brought to KID with a week of healing childcare
- **$500** can sponsor a respite care support event, giving new caregivers the support and resources they need to become self-sufficient

A better life for a child. A brighter future for our community. Thank you!

Name:_____

Address:_____

City:_____

State/Zip:_____ Phone:_____

Please accept my gift to help the children in the amount of:
○ $25 ○ $50 ○ $75 ○ Other $_____

I enclose: ○ Check (made payable to Kids In Distress)

Please charge my card:
○ VISA ○ MasterCard ○ American Express ○ Discover

Card Number:_____ Exp. Date:_____

Or: make your donation securely online at **www.kidinc.org/Fall2011**.

○ I want to do even more for the children! Please charge my credit card in the amount of $_____ each month.

○ Please send me information on how to remember Kids In Distress in my Will.

○ I'd like to receive communications from KID via email. My email address is:_____

A copy of the official registration and financial information may be obtained from the Division of Consumer Services by calling toll-free 1-800-435-7352. Registration does not imply endorsement, approval or recommendation by the state. Kids In Distress registration number is CH-218. **Your donation may be tax-deductible under section 501(c)(3) of the IRS code.**

Main Campus I Broward County
819 NE 26th Street, Fort Lauderdale, FL 33305
Phone: **954-390-7654**

Palm Beach County
5861 Heritage Park Way, Delray Beach, FL 33445
Phone: **561-272-9619**

Kids In Distress protects the privacy of the children we help. As such, names and

Copywriter: Lisa Sargent | Design: Sandie Collette, S. Collette Design
Client: Kids In Distress

9. **Grateful Newsletter Tip #9:** Add one last thank you on the reply envelope. (Yes, you should include a reply envelope, postage-paid.)

One example:

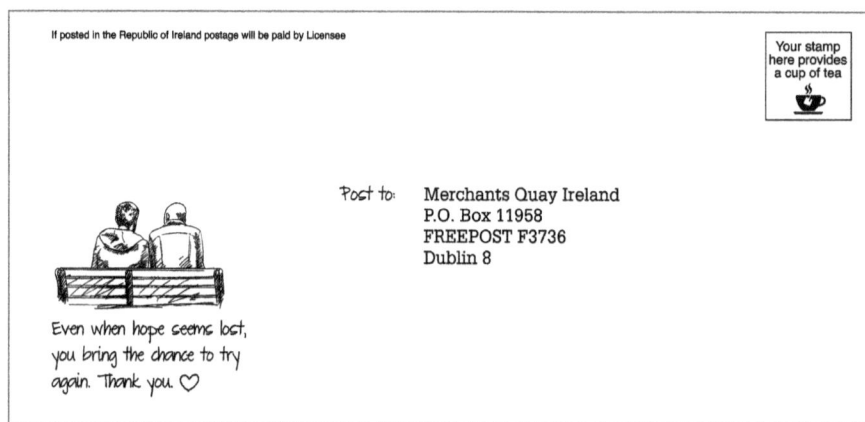

If posted in the Republic of Ireland postage will be paid by Licensee

Your stamp here provides a cup of tea

Post to: Merchants Quay Ireland
P.O. Box 11958
FREEPOST F3736
Dublin 8

Even when hope seems lost, you bring the chance to try again. Thank you. ♡

Copywriter: Lisa Sargent | Design: Sandie Collette, S. Collette Design
Client: MQI (Merchants Quay Ireland)

10. **Grateful Newsletter Tip #10:** : And don't forget to cross channels. (Yes, your newsletters can live online in archives.) For lots of our clients, we send out a simple email that lets their online subscribers know when a new print newsletter is out. The web version lives online in a newsletter archive, so they can click through to read just in case they aren't opted in to receiving mail. The email always invites them to receive the newsletter free by mail as well – which you'll remember from back in Chapter 4 is important, because multi-channel donors give more and stay longer.

Here's an example of an email, which you'll note has a "Dear Friends" salutation. We always personalize wherever possible, and you should too. And always thank!

Where love speaks a language all its own: Don't miss your latest ChildVision Newsletter...

ChildVision
National Education Centre for Blind Children

Dear Friends of ChildVision,

What do a therapy horse turned unicorn... big news for braille readers... and little learners with sight loss have in common?

Your love and support!

And this month – February – in honour of the month of love, we've a very special Winter Newsletter for you, filled with stories of hope, joy, and triumph for children with blindness in Ireland.

Coming to you with gratitude and love, don't miss your latest ChildVision newsletter, ready for reading online now:

READ THE STORIES

Speaking of love, be sure to turn to page 2 of your newsletter for what may be the greatest gifts you can give to honour the ones you love this Valentine's Day... or any day.

Because the truth is, for children and young people with severe sight loss in Ireland, your love speaks a language all its own at ChildVision.

We'd be lost without friends like you.

Remember to join everyone participating in the Step Through March Facebook Challenge by walking 10k steps a day in March to help raise vital funds for ChildVision.

Copywriter: Lisa Sargent | Design: Sandie Collette, S. Collette Design
Client: ChildVision

A final word. It's important to note that <u>all</u> these examples are performers, with some donor newsletter mailings earning returns on investment as high as 7:1 (seven dollars donated for every one dollar spent). Many also see double-digit response rates (one of the samples is from a newsletter mailing that achieved a 21% response rate!), spark legacy donations, boost retention, and move donors to come to tours and events.

In other words, it's well worth thanking donors in your newsletters.

11

In case you're not yet ready to call it a gratitude report:
The grateful annual report

> "Start where you are.
> Use what you have.
> Do what you can."
>
> — **Arthur Ashe**

Nowadays there are lots of nonprofits dead set on ditching their donor recognition lists, stripping the title of "annual report" from their annual report, and changing the name to a gratitude report or donor impact report.

Gratitude reports, especially, often read differently than the annual reports sent to public funders, corporate supporters, some private donors, and the like.

Sometimes, for example, you'll see gratitude reports walking the donor through the story of just a single beneficiary, with full and effusive focus on the donor having made the victory possible – and they often demand a special breed of buy-in from leadership.

This chapter isn't about pitting one title or type of report against the other.

Like the rest of this book, it's about incorporating gratitude in practical ways. Baby steps that become big leaps, if you will.

So even if you might never get a gratitude report across the line... or you need to adhere to certain reporting requirements of grantmakers and statutory funders... <u>and</u> you want your staff to know the role they play too... and you only have the budget for one report that has to wear all those hats...

... This chapter is for you.

Yes, you can still call it an annual report.

Yes, you can bring your good work to life for all your intended readers.

And yes, you can thank your supporters with heart and joy. You can even still include key financials and a donor honor roll.

Meet Kids In Distress, Annual Report 2012. (Yes, 2012.)

It has a lot of years under its belt now, I realize.

But I chose KID's grateful annual report to be our guide in this chapter for one important reason...

<u>So you can see what's possible when *not* everything is perfect.</u>

When Annual Report has to be the title, and you need to be creative about doing your best within a budget.

That's the nonprofit world my design colleague Sandie and I often find ourselves working in – and if you're in that world too, that's A-OK.

Here's what I mean:

- ♥ To complete this project, we were still required to use phrases like "Operational Statistics."

- ♥ There was no yielding on including a donor honor roll that listed <u>all</u> of KID's $1,000+ donors.

- ♥ There was <u>zero</u> budget for an illustrator. Oh, and we had to use stock photos for many of the images.

Still, compared to what you often find in annual reports – the Institutional-Speak, the buzzwords like "enabling efficiency" and "impact transparency," and the lonely, context-less pie charts, <u>this</u> annual report moved donor gratitude to a much happier neighborhood.

<u>We stand forever in gratitude to CEO Mark Dhooge for letting this sail across the line with his blessing, and for his generosity in granting permission for me to share it all these years later. In Mark's words:</u>

"I remember that piece well and still look back on it as one of our best. We are absolutely proud of the metrics contained within the report, many of which our programs continue to meet...[and] while KID has grown and transformed, our core values have remained the same."

Now let's unpack how we moved that thankology meter for the Kids In Distress (KID) annual report, and how your annual report can do the same.

To their credit, KID was on board with dedicating the annual report to donors, foster parents, public funders, and more.
This provided a mental anchor and freed us to thank everywhere.
Starting with the cover:

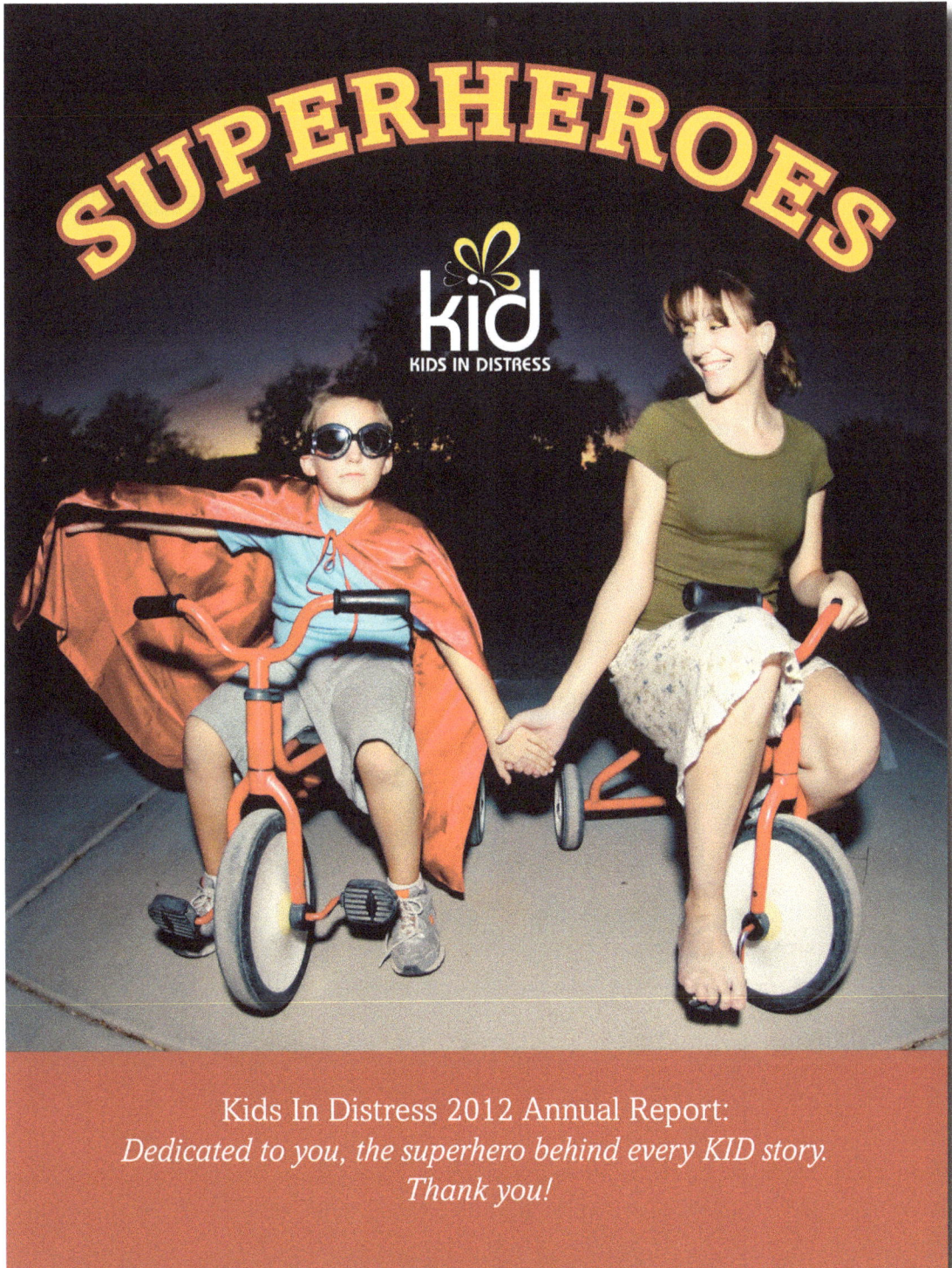

SUPERHEROES

kid
KIDS IN DISTRESS

Kids In Distress 2012 Annual Report:
Dedicated to you, the superhero behind every KID story.
Thank you!

Copywriting: Lisa Sargent | Design: Sandie Collette, S. Collette Design
Client: KID

It went on to open with the mission, values, and vision page – folding donors into the very heart of the organization from the start:

Thank you for believing in the children of Kids In Distress.

Because of heroes like you, KID provides urgently needed services to more than 10,000 children and families in South Florida every year. To this day we're still guided by the same principles on which we were founded in 1976:

MISSION

The mission of Kids In Distress is to prevent child abuse, preserve the family and treat children who have been abused and neglected.

VALUES

Family. Trust. Compassion. Safety. Wisdom. Tenacity. We don't just share our values — we live them.

VISION

A community of safe and healthy children in loving families. Safe, healthy, loving. We can't think of anything more wonderful. Can you?

Copywriting: Lisa Sargent | Design: Sandie Collette
Client: KID

And continued with the president's letter from Mark, dedicating the entire annual report to all who made KID's work possible:

You are the SUPERHERO in their stories. And ours...

Dear Friends,

This Annual Report is dedicated to you.

You, the donor. You, the foster parent. You, the corporate partner. The adoptive family. Public funder. Foundation. Board member. Volunteer. You.

For children in South Florida who have been abused and neglected – for families who are struggling – you are the reason we can help. Right here. Right now.

Partner. Friend. Collaborator. Supporter. You are all of these. And much more...

You are the shining superhero behind every KID story. *Our hero, too.*

KID President/CEO Mark Dhooge (left) paints alongside Florida Panthers' star defenseman and happy volunteer, Ed Jovanovski, during the Designing Spaces overhaul at Kids In Distress (story page 7).

It's true the economy could be (far) better. True too that as we face still deeper government cuts in the months ahead, more children and families need our help – and in more heartbreaking ways than ever before. In fact, in the coming year, we're now on track to serve over 10,000 children and families – an increase of nearly 25 percent.

But because of you, the transformative work of Kids In Distress continued uninterrupted throughout all of 2012 ... from emergency shelter for a girl who'd been locked away for twelve (yes, twelve) years, to a happy forever home for a tiny baby who was born exposed to street drugs and facing withdrawal.

Brave kids. Important kids. And each one, like you, with the heart of a hero.

Read their stories on the pages that follow. Learn about the programs that changed their lives. And know this: with you as the wind beneath their wings (or keeping aloft those trusty hero capes!) there is nothing they can't achieve.

What remarkable work you make possible here at Kids In Distress.

Thank you for being our superhero,

Mark Dhooge

Mark Dhooge
President/CEO, Kids In Distress

1

Copywriting: Lisa Sargent | Design: Sandie Collette, S. Collette Design
Client: KID

Then came the stories on the very first pages of the report itself, introduced via "A trio of triumphant stories" subhead:

It's important for you to note here that the stories we used in this section were repurposed directly from donor newsletters we'd done for KID that year, saving them time and money in gathering totally new content.

Since then, we've done the same across a bunch of annual reports – and you can too.

You are the **STARS** in their sky.

LIVES YOU CHANGED IN 2012: A TRIO OF TRIUMPHANT TRUE STORIES

Through Kids In Distress, you support the most life-changing, life-affirming work in the world. And if ever you doubt that – even for a moment – read this trio of true stories. Because without you, none would have unfolded the way they did…

ISAIAH

He was born in October 2010. Just like thousands of other babies in South Florida. Only this child was different.

Isaiah was born addicted. And while other newborns were safely nestled in their parents' arms, Isaiah was suffering from drug withdrawal.

His birth mother had used street drugs while he was still in the womb – *the term for babies like Isaiah is substance-exposed.* But to see what these infants endure… is something else altogether. To watch withdrawal pains rack their bodies. To hear the high-pitched cries. To feel powerless.

Isaiah stayed 19 days and nights in the hospital. That's where you come in.

Immediately after leaving the hospital, he was brought to Kids In Distress. Here, two KID-trained foster parents were waiting to welcome him into their loving home with open arms. He attended KID's Preschool Plus from the beginning.

Of the experience, Foster Dad John says, *"Kids In Distress was extremely welcoming. They were helpful. We could tell it was a team environment."* Better yet, Isaiah's foster family officially became his forever family! They adopted him in May.

Isaiah still attends our Preschool Plus. He's thriving. He turned two this October! And thanks to your support of KID, this birthday was filled with health, happiness and hope.

Copywriting: Lisa Sargent | Design: Sandie Collette, S. Collette Design | Client: KID
(Note: image intentionally blurred for anonymity.)

Two other key annual report sections that are noteworthy here are programs & services, and financial statements:

In most reports these sections are, well, *reported*. Proclaimed, without framing. But if you pause from the way it's always been done and remember there's a funder or a donor or a corporate partner or volunteer reading that information, as a thankologist you start wondering if there's a more inspiring way to communicate required details.

The answer, as you see below, is yes.

<u>You</u> are the wind beneath their wings, and <u>these</u> are the programs & services your generosity supported. Now won't those descriptions of the programs & services take on new meaning? Yes indeed.

You are the WIND beneath their wings.

KID PROGRAMS & SERVICES YOUR GENEROSITY SUPPORTED IN 2012

Copywriting: Lisa Sargent | Design: Sandie Collette, S. Collette Design
Client: KID

The financial statements section got the same treatment.

Our aim was to connect the annual report reader/recipient to the financial strength and stability they'd see on the page, with stock images of superhero kids on both the income statement and balance sheet as gratitude and reinforcement for the work. You can absolutely do the same for your organization.

Like this:

Copywriting: Lisa Sargent | Design: Sandie Collette, S. Collette Design | Client: KID

Another key point is the word annual. Instead of being drudgery, how can you report back on the work of the year, in a way that's true to you?

You want even corporate funders and grantmakers to know they're supporting an organization filled with life and professionalism and caring. That their "impact" goes beyond dollars and cents, to heart and soul.

For Kids in Distress, we made supporters the candle on their cake:

You are the CANDLES on our cake.

THE YEAR 2012 IN REVIEW, MADE POSSIBLE BY YOU

It's simple. Without you, KID couldn't be here. Your support sustains us. And in 2012 – whether you raced a duck or rode a bike or pledged your time or gave a donation – you made magic happen for children in South Florida who have been abused and neglected...

OF ONE-OF-A-KIND ARTWORKS COMPLETED (BY ONE-OF-A-KIND KID ARTISTS!): 2,000

OF OVERHAULS FOR KID BY TV'S "DESIGNING SPACES": 1 FABULOUS NEW ACTIVITY SPACE!

OF MILES PEDALED FOR KID BY BIGHEARTED BICYCLISTS: 25,000

Copywriting: Lisa Sargent | Design: Sandie Collette, S. Collette Design
Client: KID

And celebrated staff expertise (with the bonus of boosting credibility and trust for funders):

GOLD STAR STAFF EMPLOYEES OF THE YEAR

Gold Star Staff:
HAVE YOU HEARD?

KID staff supervisors have an average of ten years' experience – with over 100 years combined among supervisors and directors. And childcare workers at KID's Emergency Shelter have an average tenure of more than eight years. That's dedication!

Earning Your Trust Every Day

Kids In Distress has been recognized with the following awards and certifications for its exceptional community service and exemplary standards:

- Expedited accreditation by COA (Council on Accreditation) through August 2014, for upholding the highest standard of care and administrative integrity
- Florida Gold Seal Accreditation for the Kids In Distress Preschool Plus (Approved Voluntary Prekindergarten VPK provider)
- Special recognition from Broward County Sheriff's Office for KID FIRST and Family Reunification Services
- Best Abuse Prevention Program by *South Florida Parenting* magazine
- Congressional Angels In Adoption Award for KID's innovative approach to adoption

Copywriting: Lisa Sargent | Design: Sandie Collette, S. Collette Design
Client: KID

My overall point in showing you all this is, your current annual report might have – *probably does have* – some institutional-sounding edges.

<u>And that could just be what you have to work with</u>.

But you now know that things don't have to be perfect to deliver a far more grateful annual report that acknowledges donors for the generous people they are, includes the financial and programs data you need to include, and still draws larger funders deeper into your cause in a human, openhearted way.

Yes, you can even keep your donor honor roll:

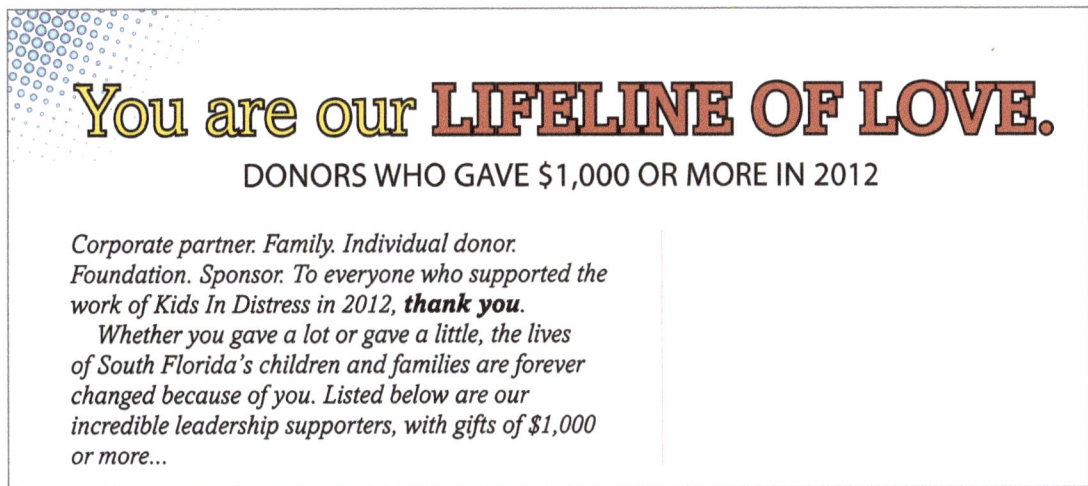

You are our LIFELINE OF LOVE.

DONORS WHO GAVE $1,000 OR MORE IN 2012

*Corporate partner. Family. Individual donor. Foundation. Sponsor. To everyone who supported the work of Kids In Distress in 2012, **thank you**.*
   Whether you gave a lot or gave a little, the lives of South Florida's children and families are forever changed because of you. Listed below are our incredible leadership supporters, with gifts of $1,000 or more...

Copywriting: Lisa Sargent | Design: Sandie Collette, S. Collette Design
Client: KID

To quote Arthur Ashe:
Start where you are. Use what you have. Do what you can.

Including, sometimes, when your client has <u>zero budget</u> for an illustrator... but you really, really, REALLY want handwritten font and drawings around that stock photo.

So, you and your designer get crafty and make your own homespun magic.

All the way down to the almost last page... and yes, I hand-drew the icons and the handfont is my own. Both made official by Designer Sandie:

Copywriting: Lisa Sargent | Design: Sandie Collette, S. Collette Design | Client: KID

Up next? Better thanking in your fundraising appeals.

CHAPTER

12

The grateful appeal:
Yes, you really can thank in an appeal

"When you do the common things in life in an uncommon way, you will command the attention of the world."

— **George Washington Carver**

If you're writing appeals and you're not thanking your donors in those letters, you're missing the boat.

Because you can absolutely honor your donors' commitment to your cause and weave gratitude into your fundraising appeals without diminishing the need for help or the urgency for continued support.

To your donors, your communications are a continuum... seen more like a conversation than stand-alone mailings, emails, etc.

What do I mean?

... *I mean you're writing to Dr. Ruiz,* who gave $100 a few months back and who's supported you through thick and thin. She deserves to know that you continue to recognize and appreciate that fact.

... I mean you're writing to Mr. Marshall, who gives $50 every time you write because he has a deeply personal connection to your work. He should continually feel seen, too.

... In fact, <u>*all your donors*</u> deserve gratitude in every fundraising letter you write.

Here are just a few of the real-world ways you accomplish this:

1. <u>**At the end of the letter, you can thank donors for reading:**</u>

   "Thank you for finding a moment to read my letter today."

2. <u>**In the body of the letter, you can preface what you're about to say as implied thanks:**</u>

   "It is in honor of your remarkable commitment that I speak openly now."

3. <u>**You can reinforce what they've made possible, then say thank you for that:**</u>

   "None of this would be possible without your generous funding of our work. You're there in every victory, and I'm grateful every day you're with us."

4. <u>**You can thank supporters for making work to date possible, then describe it:**</u>

   "For the past xx years, your unequivocal concern and commitment have contributed to victories that once, I hardly dared dream were possible:"

5. <u>**You can weave in the thanks as part of the story:**</u>

   "As a true supporter of [Nonprofit Name], you have my profound thanks for all you have done and all you do. Today I ask you to stand with us once again."

6. **<u>You can add it to the early paragraphs before the ask</u>:**

"Before I share the incredible news, before I pause to simply say Thank You, let me be clear – [Name of Nonprofit] still needs you."

{Note: The letter does go on to say thank you, and uses phrases like: *"With your great generosity at their backs, they've risked their lives to [etc.]"* and *"Together we have shown the world that [etc.]"*}

7. **<u>You can thank in advance</u>:**

"Thank you, in advance, for caring. I hope to hear from you soon."

<u>A quick note about "thank you in advance."</u> Many fundraisers loathe it. I use it sparingly. Like a strong spice, it has its time and place.

But because thankologists must be about heart and science, it's well worth noting that Neuromarketing reported on a study examining the closings of 350,000 emails. <u>These were not fundraising emails</u>. But they did ask for advice or help.

The study found that *"Thanks in advance"* yielded the highest response rate, at 65.7%[29].

"I can only say thank you... to all who give their love, their talents, and their lives for the betterment of others – working on behalf of people like me who are too old to be involved actively."

— **Real-life donor feedback**

---

29 "The Exact Three Words That Maximize Email Results," by Roger Dooley, Neuromarketing, https://www.neurosciencemarketing.com/blog/articles/email-3-closing-words.htm.

13

Advanced thanking:
Because you know you want to

"The audience does not tune themselves to you – you need to tune your message to them."

— **Nancy Duarte,** *Resonate: Present Visual Stories That Transform Audiences*

I don't have to tell you, thankologist, you already know it.

The competition for your donors' attention is increasing.

So once you've mastered the basics on thank-you letters, how do you stay ahead of the curve? Here are seven smart ways:

1. **You can incorporate quotes, rhymes, and story into your thank-yous.**

For example:

💙 <u>Quotes:</u> use a gratitude-themed poetry verse or inspirational quote from a famous author, or a beautiful quote from a beneficiary

---

Adventist Health | **St. Helena Hospital Foundation**

10 Woodland Road
St. Helena, CA 94574
707.963.6208 Phone
707.967.5620 Fax
supportercare@shhfoundation.org
www.shhfoundation.org
Tax ID # 20-1384250

Name(s)
Address1
Address2
City, State ZIP

Wherever the art of medicine is loved, there is also a love of humanity.

—Hippocrates, ancient Greek physician

<<Date>>

Dear <<Mrs. Sample>>,

His words were simple, but from the heart.

In the Intensive Care Unit of Adventist Health St. Helena, Dr. Gregory Rosellini, MD had labored for 48 hours straight just to keep his patient alive.

"When we got Danielle back," he said, "I was almost in tears."

Today you have shown that same love for health and humanity through your generous gift of <$AMOUNT> to St. Helena Hospital Foundation.

<u>Thank you for taking the time to give</u>... and thank you for helping keep world-class

---

Copywriting: Lisa Sargent | Design: Sandie Collette, S. Collette Design
Client: Glen Newhart, CFRE, Adventist Health St. Helena Hospital Foundation
(Remember supportercare@ instead of info@ as a contact in the letterhead? See above. ☺)

💙 <u>Rhyme:</u> I once wrote a thank-you that started this way:

"They may be blind. They may be small. But your kindness and generosity are helping children who live with severe sight loss... one and all."

Rhyme, along with alliteration (courage and compassion, kindness and concern), euphony, and loads of others, are literary devices our brain loves. If you can stay on-tone and appropriate – <u>NOT</u> cutesy – give it a try[30].

---

30 I write and teach about the literary devices I use in my own fundraising creative framework. This free article will get you started: https://lisasargent.com/6-ways-to-use-stylistic-and-literary-devices-to-connect-with-your-donors-on-a-deeper-level.

♥ <u>Story</u>: Return to the story you started in the appeal, and in your thank-you, bring closure. Here's one from the emergency rescue of nearly two dozen abused and abandoned horses:

Dear <<Salutation,>>   <<DATE>>

Once, they hung their noble heads in shame and pain and sadness.

Today they graze in soft, green pastures. Bodies healed and healing. Eyes bright. Spirits strong … scars receding.

When the phone rings again at   , <u>your recent donation</u> will be there to answer the call for another abused horse or donkey and bring them into loving, caring hands. Your name will be on the breeze, sweet with the scent of fresh hay and cool water.

Thank you beyond measure for your wonderful, thoughtful, generous gift of <<$AMOUNT>> to help answer the rescue call for abused horses and donkeys.

We will always remember what you've done this day.

Copywriting: Lisa Sargent

The rest of the letter is devoted to an update on the story, after which we broaden to include all the essentials you now know are needed in a thank-you.

2. You can acknowledge the basic qualities of a generous person's identity:

♥ Thank you for being the kind of person who...
♥ Because you are someone who...
♥ As a faithful supporter to XYZ charity, you have shown you are someone who...
♥ Thank you for being a donor to XYZ charity...

When it comes to donor identities, *To be* is a superhero. The simple reason is that we all want to belong... to be part of something.

In an interview with *The New York Times*[31], philanthropic psychologist Jen Shang shared that when charities randomly selected two words from a list of nine identity adjectives, then used

---

31 "Getting Into a Benefactor's Head," David Wallis. *The New York Times*, November 8, 2012. https://www.nytimes.com/2012/11/09/giving/understanding-donor-behavior-to-increase-contributions.html

them in a fundraising appeal, women increased their giving by
<u>ten percent</u>.

As you'll see, the nine identity words are joined at the hip
with "to be," used by Americans – said Shang of her research – to
describe a person who is moral. They are:

- 💔 Kind
- 💔 Caring
- 💔 Compassionate
- 💔 Helpful
- 💔 Friendly
- 💔 Fair
- 💔 Hard-working
- 💔 Generous
- 💔 Honest

Shang also found three more words that help inspire men to give.
They are:

- 💔 Strong
- 💔 Responsible
- 💔 Loyal

The fascinating work of Jen Shang and Adrian Sargeant
continues around donor identities, and at their Institute for
Sustainable Philanthropy, they've built an entire (and superb: I took
it) 8-week certificate course for fundraisers around philanthropic
psychology that you can enroll in (visit https://www.philanthropy-
institute.org.uk/ for more). In Appendix IV of this book, I share 50
donor identities and qualities you can adapt and use for your own.

3. You can dress up a thank-you letter for the holidays, or after an acquisition campaign:

According to multiple sources, about a third of all annual
giving occurs in the month of December. In my work with clients,
we've found that the holidays are also the time when monthly

donors most often choose to make a special, additional gift.

So if you're sending a letter at that time, why not look at the actual stationery you're using, and sprinkle a bit more of the magic of the season?

Here's another example of that special thank-you letterhead you saw in the early pages of this book – we also festoon the outer envelope in similar ways:

Copywriting: Lisa Sargent | Design: Sandie Collette, S. Collette Design
Client: ChildVision

4. **You can repurpose bits and pieces (a.k.a. *micro-content*) from your thank-you letters and newsletter stories to thank your supporters on social media:**

I include social media in the Advanced Thanking section because getting things right first with your thank-you letters, donation confirmation page, email thank-yous, and donor newsletters matters more.

And, like at pretty much every nonprofit on the planet, resources at Merchants Quay Ireland are limited. So in addition to their own brand of genius, MQI's communications team adapts some of what gets sent in direct mail and email, and upcycles it for social media.

I'll share a few quick examples of how that looks:

This is an Instagram thank-you going out to supporters at Christmastime thanking them once more for funding a year of Sunday dinners at the beginning of the year:

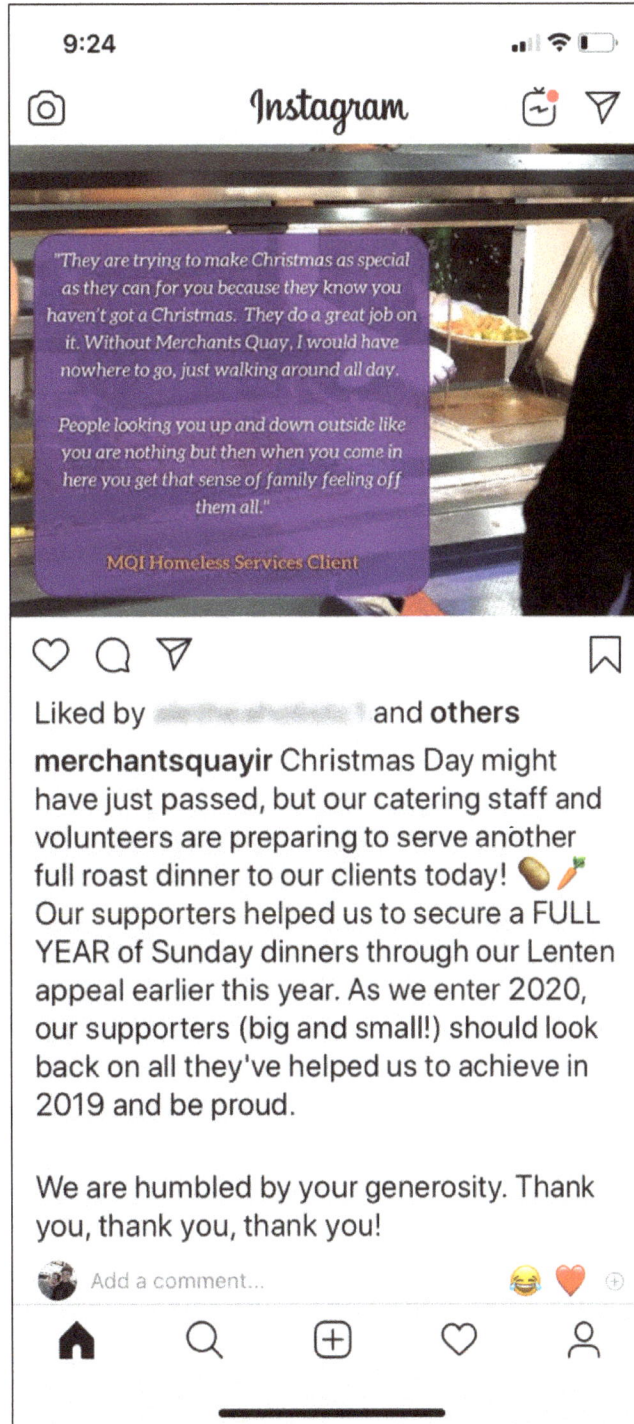

"They are trying to make Christmas as special as they can for you because they know you haven't got a Christmas. They do a great job on it. Without Merchants Quay, I would have nowhere to go, just walking around all day.

People looking you up and down outside like you are nothing but then when you come in here you get that sense of family feeling off them all."

MQI Homeless Services Client

Liked by ~~...~~ and **others**

merchantsquayir Christmas Day might have just passed, but our catering staff and volunteers are preparing to serve another full roast dinner to our clients today! 🥔🥕 Our supporters helped us to secure a FULL YEAR of Sunday dinners through our Lenten appeal earlier this year. As we enter 2020, our supporters (big and small!) should look back on all they've helped us to achieve in 2019 and be proud.

We are humbled by your generosity. Thank you, thank you, thank you!

Add a comment...

Here's another thanking supporters for sending back messages and cards during the holidays:

And a reminder: while YOU may see each media channel as separate and distinct – you may even have different teams to handle different parts of it – remember that to your donors it's still The Channel of You. Your organization.

So whether you're thanking or reporting, always be working to maintain a recognizable and consistent voice across all your donor facing channels. Your supporters will love you all the more for it.

5. You can "pre-thank" your donors to prime them for future giving:

In Part IV of this book I will introduce you to the full story of Food for the Poor's Angel Aloma, and the astounding results of a "pre-thank" test he conducted.

> For right now, the nutshell version goes like this:
>
> At the beginning of the year, Food for the Poor sent a simple thank-you card to 25,000 of its highest donors. The card was sent in an envelope. There was no ask. No reply piece. No reply envelope.
>
> By the end of the year both the major givers who'd received the card, and those who hadn't, had given nearly the same number of gifts.

But the group that received the thank-you card gave almost $450,000 more.

Angel Aloma is not alone.

In The Philanthropy Centre's epic (free) report on the role of donor acknowledgments, *Learning to Say Thank You*[32], an all-star team of "generosity researchers" including Jen Shang and Adrian Sargeant found that frequent donors who received either a CEO-centered thank-you ("So today, I want to thank you," "I want to tell you how much your commitment to IPTV means.") or a donor-centered thank-you ("You are wonderful. Really. You are.") before they received a renewal appeal were 14% to 17% more likely to renew than the no-pre-thank control group. There was no ask at all in this pre-thank.

6. You can build an entire mailing to your donors around gratitude:

Irish charity Trócaire is a steadfast force for global good and a champion of justice and equality. Because both the organization and many of its supporters have faith-based roots, Trócaire softens its fundraising during one month of the year, Missions Month in October.

---

32 "Learning to Say Thank You: The Role of Donor Acknowledgments," The Philanthropy Centre September 2018, Jen Shang, Adrian Sargeant, Kathryn Carpenter, Harriet Day. https://www.philanthropy-institute.org.uk/reports-sign-up

The charity, though, really wanted a way it could still connect with donors and show them how integral they were to the work. So together with their stellar fundraising team, Designer Sandie and I came up with a mailing that all of us now affectionately call "The Gratitude Pack." (See bird's-eye view at right.)

Next and last up in this section on Advanced Thanking, let's turn our attention to the use of Big Numbers in fundraising – and get ready for some unexpected news.

7. You can shatter the myth of Big Numbers:

If you're familiar with fundraising philosophy, you already know that you MUST, as a fundraising communicator, tell the Story of One.

By the Story of One, I mean you need to harness 'the identifiable victim effect'[33] rather than focus on vast faceless numbers (500,000 people who've been displaced by war, for example – and I'm with you, for the record: 'identifiable victim effect' has a terrible sound to it).

With that said, however, there is now evidence that suggests there are times when introducing vastness may be a good thing.

In the Institute for Sustainable Philanthropy's *Learning How to Say Thank You*, Jen Shang and her generosity research team found that:

"When an individual story is highly emotional, additional information on vastness can serve to enhance donor wellbeing. So, for example, donors can also be thanked for the difference they will make over an extended period of time (i.e. in our test, a year not a week)..."

They go on to note that vastness of mission, in organizations where

---

33 Per Wikipedia's excellent definition, the "identifiable victim effect" refers to the tendency of individuals to offer greater aid when a specific, identifiable person ("victim") is observed under hardship, as compared to a large, vaguely defined group with the same need. https://en.wikipedia.org/wiki/Identifiable_victim_effect To read more about one study around this, *Dan Ariely's The Upside of Irrationality* explains it wonderfully.

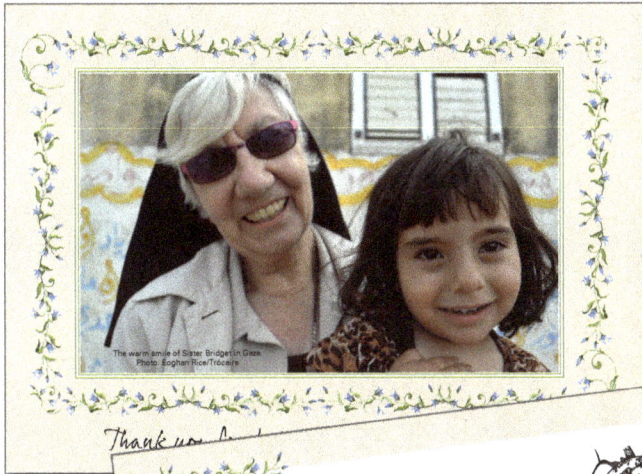

"Medicine. Knowing someone out there cares...From the bottom of my heart, thank you for standing with us."
— Sister Bridget Tighe, Trócaire partner in Jerusalem and Gaza

...TSTEPS OF MISSIONARIES

...of antiquity, missionaries across this island
...to the en...
...arth to help people caught
...r poverty... war... famine...
...risis. Today Trócaire staff
...carry that message of
...sion of love in action.
...wn to the children,
...nly thanks to your help,
...ging hope and
...e world.

...us,

...6AD   T: +44 (0)28 90 808030   E: infoni@trocaire.org...
...h in Ireland and a mem...

Because of you, Trócaire partner Sister Bridget can tend to Gaza's desperately sick and wounded. Thank you. Photo: Trócaire

POSTAL GROUP
TWO

Delivered by
Royal Mail
C9 10004

From Jerusalem and Gaza,
from the heart of Trócaire,
Sister Bridget's uplifting words
of thanks for you...

Sister Bridget Tighe's simple message of thanks for you from Jerusalem and Gaza is so beautiful that this month, it bears repeating...

"Your kindness makes more of a difference than you know. Food. Medicine. Knowing someone out there cares.

The situations are desperate. But Trócaire supporters bring people comfort and care, and keep staff and partners like me strong. Thank you for standing with us."

I can think of no better way to honour your generosity than with those words of gratitude from Jerusalem and Gaza.

You and I know all too well that Gaza is one of the world's most war-torn places. But you can see by the front of this card that hope still lives there.

Hope lives, because of _you_, a steadfast supporter to Trócaire.

Because of the medicine you bring to the little children who cry from intestinal worms. Because of the care you deliver to people young and old who have been maimed in the bombings. Because of your support for Sister Bridget.

You make this work happen not only in Gaza. You are there for people who feel utterly forgotten in over twenty of the hardest-hit countries on earth.

And just like the people of Ireland did when they set forth from this fair island on those missions of mercy so long ago, you carry a message of hope:

"You are not forgotten. We are here to help. And here we will stay, until your long night of fear is over. You are not forgotten. Love will conquer fear."

This month and every month, <u>thank you for being the heart of Trócaire</u>,

Caoimhe de Barra

Caoimhe de Barra
CEO, Trócaire

P.S.   I wish you could see how tireless staff and partners are, wherever they work in your honour. But this month, especially, would you use the small reply enclosed to send a message of love and strength back to Sister Bridget in Gaza? Conditions are so dispiriting, and your words will really lift her up. Thank you so much for caring.

Trōcaire

Photos of people being helped by...
from top left: Maria (9), with her mother...
Guatemala; Wife Betty and husband Joe...
with his mother Aysha, in Gaza; schoolc...
people, in Myanmar. Photo credits, Tróc...
Morrillo, Niamh McCarthy, Mark Stedma...

UNTIL L...

Trócaire is the overseas development agency of...
their lives, meet their basic needs and ensure the...
ROI Charity Regulatory Authority No. 2000...

"YOU ARE NOT FORGOTTEN
SISTER BRIDGET IN GAZ...

Every day at Trócaire, staff, partners, an...
world's hardest-hit places. This month, in...
who sees such dispiriting conditions...

Addressee
Address line 1
Address line 2
Address line 3
Mailing City
Mailing Cou...
Postcode

We'd like to continue secu...
donations have changed...

If you prefer not to rec...
here...

If you'd like to bec...
call us at the num...
and decrease supp...
organisation or c...

(When R...

...kindness,
...ow small,
...sted."
— Aesop

Copywriting: Lisa Sargent | Design: Sandie Collette, S. Collette Design
Client: Trócaire

highly emotional stories can't be used, can "still translate to wellbeing if it can be linked to donor connection with the organization and their passion for the cause."[34]

Here's one more finding.

In their study, Shang and her team also found that – in thank-you communications – donors felt better with the longer, more abstract timeframe language than they did with the shorter, concrete timeframe.

The two timeframes they tested were one year vs. one week. As in:

Thanks to your donation, this week we did not have to turn away a single patient.

Versus:

Thanks to your donation, this year we did not have to turn away a single patient.

They found that using "year" language not only made the work seem more concrete and closer to completion, it also made donors feel better about themselves.

To learn more, I advise a thorough reading (or two!) of The Philanthropy Centre's *Learn to Say Thank You* report.

This is all just the tip of the tale.

Advanced thanking, like so much of fundraising, changes and grows every day. So that we may continue thanking donors well, it's our job as thankologists to keep pace and experiment, test, and grow alongside those changes.

The future awaits.

---

34 *"Learning to Say Thank You,"* Shang, Sargeant, et. al., pages 30-40.

PART IV:

Prove it!
Answers for fundraisers asked to "prove their case" around better thanking (and what that means)

"If you want sense, you'll have to make it yourself."

— **Norton Juster,** *The Phantom Tollbooth*

---

oh they ♡ love ♡ me

In this book so far you've already seen several examples of thank-yous from an Irish homeless and drugs services charity called Merchants Quay Ireland (MQI).

There's a very good reason for that.

Because in September 2008, with fewer than 2,000 donors on its database, MQI started overhauling the way it treated donors. (Forever hat tip to MQI's then head of fundraising, Denisa Casement, now CEO of the Casement Group.)

This included, among other things, donor-centric thank-you letters.

By 2017 they had experienced a thirteen-percentage point increase in donor retention. From 57% to 70%. And the jump wasn't due to file stagnation either.

Active acquisition meant the donor file also stood nine times higher than in 2008, at more than 18,000.

And revenue increase?

That was north of fourteen-fold[35].

Again, the thank-you letters were just one part of this. But if donor feedback is any indication, a prominent part.

---

35 "Lessons from Merchants Quay Ireland: The Resounding Eight-Year Success Story of a Donor-Based Approach to Raising (Far) More Money, for Good," by Lisa Sargent, Denisa Casement, CFRE, and Sandra Collette. Free, 47-page PDF download on my website (no sign-up needed): https://lisasargent.com/resources/.

Here are just three brief examples of what supporters say, verbatim, about how it feels to give to, and be part of, MQI:

- 💜 *"If you so much as made them a cup of tea they'd write you a letter and say thanks."*

- 💜 *"Oh, they love me!"*

- 💜 *"You just know when charities are good charities by the way they follow up on things. Not coming back makes me feel – oh. Did they get my [donation]?"[36]*

It gets better.

Because there's another reason I know investing in donor thanking is still bringing benefits to the good work of MQI.

I know because I wrote almost every one of those thank-you letters, along with appeals, emails, and newsletters, to donors. Right up to Autumn 2020.

Their donor file is now over 20,000 supporters and growing. And yes, they still regularly get "fan mail" from their donors.

I'm talking about notecards in rickety handwriting begging forgiveness for said handwriting, because the author of the letter is getting on in years and their hands shake. Letters on bits of scrap paper sharing life stories that – even if you aren't easily moved to tears – would make your eyes mist at the great good in people's hearts, at the painful struggles that move them to give and find comfort in helping others.

Many times there are donations tucked inside the envelopes to these letters.

---

36 "Meeting the needs of core supporters: interviews with Merchants Quay Ireland supporters," a 2018 study of Irish charity donors spearheaded by Mark Phillips of Bluefrog Fundraising, https://bluefroglondon.com/, and Damian O'Broin of Ask Direct, https://www.askdirect.ie/ Survey results shared permission of, and thanks to, the eternally gracious Merchants Quay Ireland. (I love you guys forever ☺.)

Which honestly? Donations, in this case, aren't the point. The point is genuine, heart-to-heart, human connection and caring and belonging.

In a perfect world, of course, you'd <u>never</u> have to "prove" the worth of thanking someone for making a donation...

... You'd never have to "prove" that saying thank you isn't cutesy, or yucky, or overbearing, or saccharine, or trite.

... You'd never have to "prove" that yes, it will be effective and it *does* matter at <u>your</u> organization, in <u>your</u> home country, for your donors.

<u>But the truth is, many of you will be required to do just that.</u>

If so, these next four chapters will give you a deluge of data and test results and research experiments... and yes, brain science... behind why it pays to invest in better thanking at your nonprofit.

My thinking is, if the real-life story of a <u>fourteen-fold increase in revenue</u> and a <u>seventy percent donor retention rate</u> with a growing file of active donors won't convince your decision-makers to immediately get behind better thanking, maybe the chapters that follow will.

You've got this, thankologist. I'm cheering for you.

Now let's build your case...

Photo: A beautiful example of what happens when you start to do donor retention communications right: real-life fan mail sent back to Merchants Quay Ireland by delighted, engaged, appreciated donors.

CHAPTER

14

The gratitude experiments:
Why naysayers are dead wrong about the power of thanking

> "Sometimes the bravest and most important thing you can do is just show up."
>
> — **Brené Brown**

In June 2018, then University of Chicago researchers Amit Kumar and Nicholas Epley conducted three experiments during which they asked participants to write gratitude letters, then predict how their letters would make the intended recipients feel.

What they discovered was remarkable indeed[37]:

1. *Senders* overestimated how awkward they would make the recipients feel.
2. *Senders* underestimated how much the letter of gratitude would mean to recipients.

---

37 Kumar, A. & Epley, N. (2018). "Undervaluing gratitude: Expressers misunderstand the consequences of showing appreciation." *Psychological Science*, 29(9), 1423-1435. Links to all of Dr. Kumar's publications are here, http://www.kumar-amit.com/research-papers/

The key element for recipients?

<u>Warmth of the letter</u>.

The results led the researchers to a conclusion they summed up so beautifully, I include it verbatim here:

"Expressing gratitude is a powerful act of civility benefitting both expressers and recipients."
— *Amit Kumar and Nicholas Epley*

<u>Kumar and Epley aren't the only researchers to show the notable effects of properly expressing thanks</u>.

In two gratitude experiments[38, 39] conducted by Francesca Gino, now a professor at Harvard Business School, and Wharton School's Adam Grant, a simple thank-you letter heightened the recipients' <u>sense of self-worth</u>.

By more than double.

And Gino and Grant's study suggests that the effects of *not* saying thank you are closely linked to a person's willingness to offer <u>future</u> support.

How *much* more willing?

You guessed it: More than double.

Gino even went so far as to say that <u>the extent of what she came to call</u> "the Gratitude Effect" was the most surprising part of her research.

When it comes to <u>not</u> thanking donors, Adrian Sargeant's timeless research report, *Managing Donor Defection*,[40] exposes similar trouble.

---

38 Leddy, Chuck. "The Power of 'Thanks,'" *The Harvard Gazette*, March 19, 2013. http://news.harvard.edu/gazette/story/2013/03/the-power-of-thanks/

39 Grant, Adam M. and Gino, Francesca. "A Little Thanks Goes A Long Way: Explaining Why Gratitude Expressions Motivate Prosocial Behavior," *Journal of Personality and Social Psychology, 2010.* https://www.umkc.edu/facultyombuds/documents/grant_gino_jpsp_2010.pdf And find more from Gino on her website: https://francescagino.com/

40 Sargeant, Adrian. "Managing Donor Defection: Why Should Donors Stop Giving?", 2001. [online; for-purchase] https://onlinelibrary.wiley.com/doi/epdf/10.1002/pf.3204

His work showed that when donors were asked their reasons for no longer supporting an organization, 13.2% came right out and said it was <u>because they hadn't been thanked</u>.

Dive deeper into Professor Sargeant's findings, and you'll see more trouble:

- **36.2%** said they felt other causes were more deserving
- **9.2%** couldn't recall supporting the organization
- **8.1%** said they hadn't been informed how their donations were used
- **5.6%** said the organization no longer needed their support.

It's not a big jump to see that in addition to the 13.2% who specifically said they left because they were never thanked, the other reasons I've just listed above are at least in some way tied to a lack of proper acknowledgment.

Which means it is entirely plausible that poor or nonexistent thanking kills the joy of giving in as many as <u>seven out of every ten donors</u> who defect. (For a free infographic courtesy of the fine folks at Bloomerang, see footnote below[41].)

Need more?

In their e-book I referenced earlier called "Learning to Say Thank You: The Role of Donor Acknowledgments" researchers Jen Shang, Adrian Sargeant, Kathryn Carpenter, and Harriet Day offer proof and testing aplenty on the might of the thank-you.

For example,[42] they found evidence that thank-yous:

- <u>Increased average gift</u>: "In a database where the average number of past overall gifts made by donors is three, a thank-you letter reaffirming the difference that their donations made increased average gifts by 60% without reducing the response rate in comparison to a control group of donors who did not receive this thank-you."

---

41 "Charities That Focus on Retention Will Change the World," Bloomerang. [online] https://bloomerang.co/blog/charities-that-focus-on-retention-will-change-the-world/
42 "Learning to Say Thank You: The Role of Donor Acknowledgments" by Jen Shang, Adrian Sargeant, Kathryn Carpenter and Harriet Day. September 2018. https://www.philanthropy-institute.org.uk/reports-sign-up

- ♥ <u>Increased goodwill</u>: "We estimated that if these thank-yous are done in a consistent and lively manner, organizations have the potential to increase the good feeling in their database by a minimum of 20% over five years."

- ♥ <u>Increased average gift, redux</u>: In one of the tests where a thank-you preceded a renewal letter by about four weeks, donors who were thanked gave $45.32 more on average than the non-thanked cohort.

As a thankologist, it's important for you to know that the source of all this gratitude goodness is not something elusive.

You can access it every time you write your letters.

That's because gratitude lights up your donor's brain. Literally.

In a study[43] that imaged brains <u>experiencing</u> gratitude, the ACC, or *anterior cingulate cortex* (the gray matter that sits a bit behind your eyebrows) and the mPFC, or *medial prefrontal cortex* (slightly upstairs from the ACC), <u>literally lit up</u>: specifically, in the areas linked to moral and value judgment, and something called "theory of mind" – the understanding of others.

By lighting up the ACC, it appears that gratitude touches a donor's emotion and memory centers ... which makes the enhanced positive feelings of those thank-you messages in Kumar and Epley's research perfectly understandable.

There's more.

Research[44] has shown that gratitude (both receiving and expressing) releases the neurotransmitters *dopamine* and *serotonin* in the brain – and some researchers point to the neuropeptide *oxytocin* as well. You may know about them as the 'feel-good' or 'happiness' brain chemicals. But there's more

---

43 "Neural Correlates of Gratitude," *Frontiers in Psychology*, https://www.frontiersin.org/articles/10.3389/fpsyg.2015.01491/full/

44 Research on gratitude's brain chemicals is broad and wide, ranging from The Wharton School to *Frontiers In Psychology*, among many, many others.

to it than that. Associated with willpower, motivation, and, in dopamine's case, reward, these chemicals increase behavior experts call *prosocial*. In other words, it moves people to 'act for the greater good,' not just their own. Yes indeed, we're talking about altruism here, thankologists... and gratitude helps open the door.

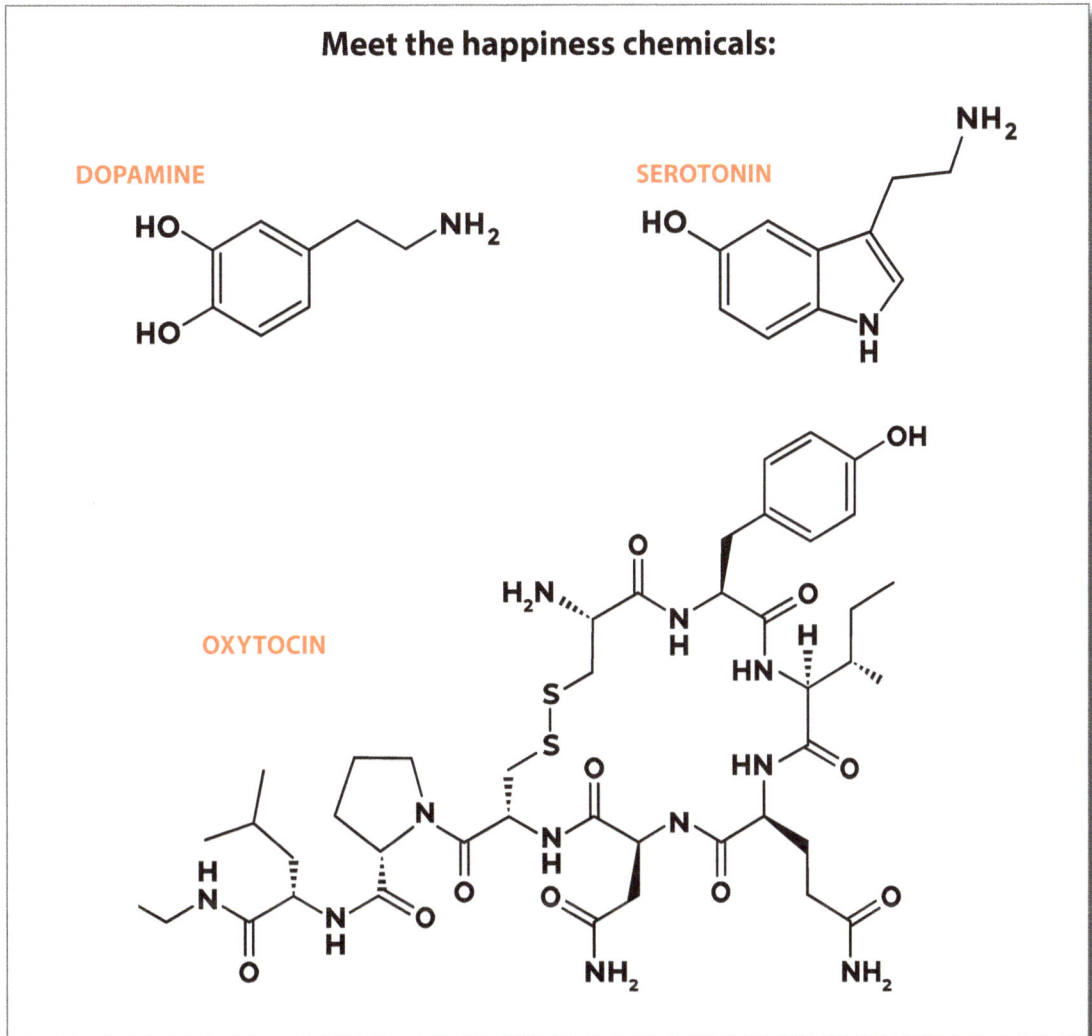

Meet the happiness chemicals:

DOPAMINE

SEROTONIN

OXYTOCIN

Want to bring it all full circle? Guess where serotonin is produced?

In our old friend, the ACC, or anterior cingulate cortex. To paraphrase deaf educator and sign language pioneer, Jean-Baptiste Massieu[45]:

---

45 Instrumental in having helped formalize French Sign Language – which in turn formed the roots of American Sign Language – Massieu's original quote is, "Gratitude is the memory of the heart." [online] https://www.disabilitymuseum.org/dhm/lib/detail.html?id=1687&&page=all (120-126) and https://en.wikipedia.org/wiki/Jean_Massieu.

**Gratitude really *is* the memory of the heart...
and the brain, too.**

Or as author Dr. John Amodeo said, people (in other words, your donors) like feeling appreciated[46] because:

1. They feel *valued*.
2. They feel *"seen."*
3. They feel *liked*.
4. It *deepens meaning* in their lives.
5. It *connects* them.

Now you have all the ammunition you need to defend investing in your donor acknowledgment program with something other than, "It's the right thing to do."

The next question is, can the timing and quality of your thank-you letters help or hinder The Gratitude Effect? Let's explore...

"I find so much hope in the work of the very many who do what is right and never lose sight of their humanity. Thank you for all that you do."

— **B.,** *a real-life donor who emailed back
this beautiful message of hope for partners in the field*

---

46 "Why We Like Being Appreciated," John Amodeo, PhD, MFT, *Psychology Today.* [online] https://www.psychologytoday.com/us/blog/intimacy-path-toward-spirituality/201604/why-we-being-appreciated

CHAPTER

15

The 48-hour question
(Or, how soon must I send... and how much does that matter?)

> *"There are few things on this earth more dangerous than waiting."*
>
> — **AJ Leon,** *Author, The Life and Times of a Remarkable Misfit*

The 48-Hour Answer

One of the most-asked questions about donor acknowledgments is this:

After having received a donation,
how soon do I need to send a thank-you letter?

Practically everyone will tell you 48 hours.

And global donor comms expert and renowned fundraising author Tom Ahern has long cited this evidence to support that 48-hour window:

"First-time donors who received a personal thank-you within 48 hours were FOUR TIMES more likely to give again.

Yes: thanking in 48 hours = 400% improvement in renewal rates." [47]

But... take note. The operative phrase Tom quotes here isn't just any old thank-you. ***It's personal thank-you.*** That's because the data also has something to say about <u>quality</u>, and the very real danger in rushing a thank-you out the door.

Speed <u>PLUS</u> Quality Matter More

In *The Seven Key Drivers of Donor Commitment Idea Bank* by The Agitator DonorVoice's Kevin Schulman, he points to their studies that show 3 out of 10 donors want a prompt thank-you.

Thirty percent.

But **fifty percent** – or 5 donors out of 10 in their studies – say <u>personalization matters more than speed</u>.

In other words, Schulman says, "you don't get points for speed" if your thank-you is devoid of heart and personalization. [48]

Kevin isn't alone.

In 2014-2015, über-fundraiser Mark Phillips and his talented crew at UK agency Bluefrog decided to take matters of thanking in hand.

To a sample of donors at one of their nonprofit clients, they tested "a (good) computer generated letter" against a highly personalized thank-you.

---

47 "How quickly should you thank a new donor?" Tom Ahern, 17 March 2016 blog post, citing Damian O' Broin of AskDirect's 2011 IFC presentation and McConkey Johnson International (now Christian Fundraising Consultancy). https://tomahern.typepad.com/my_weblog/2016/03/20-questions-the-test-donor-communications-when-you-really-dont-know.html

48 "Seven Key Drivers of Donor Commitment Idea Bank," Kevin Schulman/DonorVoice. [online, slide 8]. The principal study referenced DonorVoice's *"online, nationally (US) represented survey among 1200 recent (last 12 months), frequent (more than 2 gifts cause based charities) donors."* https://www.slideshare.net/kschulman14/donor-voice-seven-key-drivers-idea-bank-report

The group of donors that received the personalized thank-you donated **<u>sixteen percent more</u>** over the following twelve months.[49]

Last piece of research for you, released in 2022.

Growing loyalty grows income: what nearly 50,000 donors revealed

In a decade-long study, veteran nonprofit pros Roger Lawson and Richard Spencer of UK research-based consultancy About Loyalty sought to measure how supporter loyalty impacts subsequent giving. Their study tracked the responses to a series of questions on loyalty – and the subsequent giving – of nearly 50,000 donors to 30+ charities.

In their own words, Lawson and Spencer's study revealed that "growing loyalty grows income."

Resoundingly well, too:

"... just a +1-point increase in supporter loyalty over 3 years can lead to 20% more income, 15% more donors continuing to give, and 9% more legacy pledges."

Among these supporters, the team found the three most significant drivers of loyalty are: commitment, satisfaction, and trust.

<u>Trust and satisfaction are the two I want to highlight here for you.</u> <u>Namely</u>:

- ♥ **Trust** that your charity does what it promises
- ♥ **Satisfaction** with your charity's communications and fundraising

Commitment, of course, meant supporters who felt committed to a charity and its cause were more loyal. I'd be willing to bet that **trusting** a charity will do what it promises and being **satisfied** with that charity's

---

49 "Your Grandmother is a better fundraiser than you are," Mark Phillips. 11 November 2015, Queer Ideas Blog, https://queerideas.co.uk/2015/11/your-grandmother-is-a-better-fundraiser-than-you-are.html.

communications and fundraising go a long way toward driving that commitment. And investing in making sure your donors are thanked well seems like an easy first step to me. [50]

Bottom line?

Promptness matters. We're fools to think it doesn't.

But in donor thank yous, quality and personalization are <u>as dangerous to ignore</u> as speed.

My suggestion?

If it means getting a warm, personal, genuine thank-you out the door in 3 or 4 days, vs. churning out a dry-as-dust form acknowledgment in 24 or 48 hours... please, for your supporters, take an extra 1-2 days to deliver something heartfelt.

The research proves you right.

"I appreciate your quick response to a gift, love hearing about the work you do"

— Anonymized donor response (#254) to a supporter survey question on *"Why I give"*

---

50 "The definitive case for growing supporter loyalty," Roger Lawson and Richard Spencer, 2022. About Loyalty [online, free on sign-up] https://www.about-loyalty.com/report-2022.

CHAPTER

16

Clear-thinking on the format fog:
The core pieces your thank-you pack needs

"Letters are expectation packaged in an envelope."

— **Shana Alexander,** "The Surprises of the Mail," *Life* (1967)

Let me start this section on the format of a thank-you by saying you must carefully think through your choices, and with one format especially.

<u>A postcard</u>.

True story...

An organization I once wrote for that was brilliant at thanking in all other respects decided to save money by mailing postcard thank-yous to all donors who gave less than $15.

The message thanked the donor for their gift, acknowledged the amount, and had some lovely, brief sentiments included.

Feedback from supporters was less than positive.

Donors called. They wrote. They emailed. They all asked the same thing:

"Why would you broadcast my gift to the world? I don't want my mailman thinking I'm stingy. I don't want other people to know who I give to. I thought you respected me!"

Like I said, this was an organization that cared <u>a lot</u> about its donors, and still made the wrong decision for the people it was mailing to.

It goes to show how important it is to think things through when it comes to donor communications. Postcards may be stellar in some situations, it's true.

But the best format for thanking, to quote fundraising author and legend Mal Warwick[51], is "It depends."

Sometimes it's a single handwritten notecard. Or a simple letter, hand signed and nestled inside the envelope in which it arrives. Sometimes it's a special insert. Other times it could be a back-end premium (a gift that was promised in your acquisition/prospecting mailer in return for a donation). Or a letter from a beneficiary.

It depends.

In my world, the core pieces of a thank-you mailing consist of:

- An outer envelope,
- A 1-sided, 1-page thank-you letter, specific to the appeal or newsletter or occasion that prompted it,
- A reply envelope.

---

51 If you don't know about the exceptional fundraising books, work, and nonprofit career of Mal Warwick, he's someone you should learn from. Among other Warwick titles, a dog-eared, often-consulted version of his *How to Write Successful Fundraising Letters* sits in my creative studio to this day.

This doesn't mean you should resort to autopilot, ever. Before sending any thank-you, you should <u>always</u> be asking questions like these:

- 💔 What have I promised to send?
- 💔 Where am I in my conversation with this donor?
- 💔 Who am I thanking?
- 💔 Why am I thanking them?
- 💔 What was the gift (because it might not always be cash)?
- 💔 What is their giving history with us?
- 💔 What appeal prompted the gift?
- 💔 By what media channel?
- 💔 Is there something that triggered this reason to say thank you, a giving anniversary or giving threshold, for example?
- 💔 Is a basic letter and envelope the best format?
- 💔 Am I inviting them to something else as part of this? Can I?
- 💔 Do I need to generate a second letter for some reason, such as a tribute?
- 💔 Who is my signatory?
- 💔 How "warm and fuzzy" can I get?
- 💔 Do I need to include something else that's been requested, either by this individual giver (such as a legacy planner, for example), or by so many other donors that we always include it?

What should <u>you</u> include with your thank-yous then?

Again, it depends. On the recipient. On the situation. On the channel.

For virtually all my clients a basic thank-you mailing consists of a thank you letter, reply envelope, and sometimes an invitation to an upcoming event. But this is certainly not the only option you have.

Below you'll find some, but by no means all, of the common and less common pieces to consider –

1. **Thank-you letter,** obviously (usually 1-page, 1-side), or thank-you card.

2. **BRE**, Business Reply Envelope, or Freepost envelope: Postage is prepaid by, and addressed to, the mailer (your nonprofit).

3. **CRE** or Courtesy Reply Envelope: a reply envelope that has no postage and is blank in the upper right corner, or has a box that says 'Your stamp here.' My vote is <u>always</u> for BRE or Freepost (UK/ Ireland) because it's one less hurdle for your donor to leap.

4. **Reply Slip:** Most of my clients never include reply slips in their thank-yous, but they do include reply envelopes. However, other organizations do include a reply form (see Chapter 17 for more on this).

5. **Remittance envelopes:** A remittance, or wallet flap, envelope is where the reply is a flap that tears off the reply envelope. You see it a lot in private secondary schools and higher education.

6. **Other inserts:** Some organizations include additional inserts with their thank-you letters. For example:

    a. <u>Who-your-donation-is-helping photos</u>: Here in the US, I'm thinking of SmileTrain, who sends a picture of a child in its thank-yous.
    b. <u>Gratitude vignettes</u>: At one organization we used a single sheet of paper folded multiple times to create a mini booklet with "gratitude vignettes" and photos. Fondly known to us as the MBOT, or mini-book-of-thanks, donors loved it.
    c. <u>Note cards</u>: Years back, one animal welfare organization sent note cards with a reprint of one of their most famous shelter resident's front paws which the creative director personally fetched with a pet-safe ink stamp pad.
    d. <u>Lift notes</u>: A note or drawing from a beneficiary, for example, children's services might include drawings or notes from the kids.

CHAPTER

17

To ask or not to ask:
The thorniest thank-you question

> ## "I reject your reality and substitute my own!"
>
> — *The Dungeonmaster* (and popularized by Adam Savage of "Mythbusters" fame)

To Ask in a donation thank-you letter... or Not to Ask?

That, my friends, is a question that fuels churning waters of controversy.

In other words:

Should your thank-you letters include Asks — direct asks, implied asks, soft asks, or some secret combination thereof?

Or should they contain No Asks whatsoever?

The Askers say ask early, ask boldly, ask often. Including in thank-you letters.

The No-Askers say never ever in thank-yous: gratitude is open-hearted, not open-handed.

To help you decide on which side of Camp Ask you want to pitch your tent, let's examine two things:

1. The meaning of the "Ask" and its various levels;
2. Some of the arguments used by <u>both</u> sides, pro-Ask and no-Ask.

The meaning of the fundraising "Ask" and its 3 basic incarnations

When fundraisers talk about Asks, we overwhelmingly mean asking for money. Cash donations. Legacies. Sustainer gifts. Upgrades. Renewals. Etcetera.

But not always.

Sometimes the ask is an advocacy rallying cry. Or a request to send back an engagement device or a survey. Or an invitation to a donor tour.

<u>For the purposes of this discussion, when I say ask, or asking, it means for a cash contribution.</u>

Of which there are three types of Asks:

#1 The Direct Ask:

The direct ask comes right out and says what it wants. "Please can I count on your second donation of $25 or more?" "Will you please send $25." "I am also writing to ask if you will please donate $25."

#2 The Soft Ask:

Huntsinger & Jeffer's Creative Director Willis Turner once schooled me on the Soft Ask in a wonderful article in *FundRaising Success* (now *Nonprofit Pro*). According to Turner, you are probably putting Soft Asks in your thank-you letters all along without realizing it.

"Based on a long experience with clients, I think a soft ask is a good thing. The reason your donor sent you a gift in the first place is that she believes in you and wants to help. The TY letter should give her another opportunity to experience the good feeling she got from helping you the first time.

But the key word is soft. Say something like, "The continuing support of friends like you is what makes our work possible ...." [52]

Other soft asks might include: "We couldn't do this work without you." Or "It's because of you that we are able to..."

#3 The Implied Ask:

An Implied Ask doesn't come right out and say anything at all. It hints around the edges, sometimes without a lot of subtlety.

For example, by including a BRE with your thank-you, you are making an implied ask. And, depending on how you phrase the copy, a reply slip can be either a direct ask or a soft ask.

Either way, you're asking.

I am <u>not</u> implying this is a bad thing.

In fact, according to Mr. Turner's definitions, you will clearly see in the samples in this book that I use what Turner calls soft and implied asks in my thank yous <u>all the time</u>.

HOWEVER.

There is an organization in the U.S., a bit below $10 million in annual revenues, that for purposes of this book will go unnamed.

Every year this group receives approximately $250,000 in additional donations by putting direct asks in their thank-you letters. Hard ask in the letter, plus a reply slip, and a BRE.

---

52 "How to Write a Fundraising Thank You Note," by Willis Turner. *NonProfit Pro magazine*, April 21, 2014. https://www.nonprofitpro.com/post/turner-how-write-fundraising-thank-you-note/all/

But.

Their donor retention rate barely crests 20%. Abysmal. Put another way: every year they were <u>losing</u> eight out of every ten donors they'd just acquired.

Would they consider, I asked, testing a small group of new donors without the hard asks in the thank-you, at least? Tiny improvements could yield big results.

They looked at me like I'd popped out of an alien pod.

Then they just came out and said what they were not-so-secretly thinking. *"Lisa, are you @#$%^ mad?! We make $250,000 a year from those thank-yous!"*

In the end, they wouldn't let me split test. Not even a little.

Sadly, this kind of inflexibility has already started to catch up with them.

I spoke with someone who was still there, just a few years back.

As I marveled at her impressive new title, she confessed: she was one of the only experienced staff left. They were doing loads of (expensive) acquisition, but donor retention was still in the pits. Still low, low twenties. Most of the staff I knew, demoralized by the continuing donor exodus, had moved on.

Now let's look at more encouraging real-life results, complete with testing, graciously shared with *The Agitator* blog by Food for the Poor's Angel Aloma:[53]

"Thank-you letters have been effective fundraisers for our organization. On average, we get more than one-fifth of our net income from them. We pay a lot of attention to the quality and the strength of the letters and make sure they are tremendously donor-centric. We don't include any ask in the letter, but we do include [a reply] envelope and reply piece.

---

53 As featured in Roger M. Craver's superb book *Retention Fundraising*, The Agitator blog, and other sources.

Aloma goes on to elaborate on his 'pre-thank' test I described to you on page 122:

"Amongst our highest donors, we tested two groups. At the beginning of the year we sent a sincere, simple thank-you card [in an envelope; not a postcard] to 25,000 donors for their past generosity — no ask, no reply piece, no [reply] envelope. The other group didn't receive this [special thank-you]. Both groups gave almost identical numbers of gifts that year, but the group that received the thank-you gave almost $450,000 more."

If you are part of an organization that requires a direct ask for another gift in thank you letters, what donor relations author and expert Lynne Wester [54] less than lovingly refers to as a "thask," it would be wise, and potentially profitable, to find a way to at least test soft- and implied-ask or even no-ask thank yous, like Angel Aloma did.

Because a 20% donor retention rate means an 80% donor attrition rate. And that's not a goal any thankologist should aspire to. (PS. Want more on donor retention, including the staggering effect of just a 10% increase in retention over 14 years? Don't miss Appendix II of this book.)

```
"I love getting letters back on how
I have changed someone's life. I always
shed a little tear it makes me feel
so good."
```

—Anonymized donor response (#1070) to a supporter survey question on
"Anything else you'd like to share?"

---

54 If you don't know the work of Lynne Wester, you absolutely need to: Lynne's Donor Relations Group and the vast resources they share can make you a better fundraiser. Find DRG at: https://www.donorrelations.com.

A FINAL WORD:
So where do you go from here, thankologist?

---

*"Love is at the root of everything.
All learning... all relationships.
Love, or the lack of it."*

— **Fred Rogers,**
From the 2022 Netflix documentary, *Won't You Be My Neighbor*

It was an eternity ago by now.

After thirty-one seasons, spanning from 1968 to 2001, the US children's television show *Mr. Rogers' Neighborhood* ended forever.

Fred Rogers himself, the show's unassuming star – who served as host, creator, and voice to many of the characters – died two years later.

But the legacy of Fred McFeely Rogers lives on, even in this book for you.

Because in the incredible 2022 Netflix documentary made about the show, our beloved Mr. Rogers says this:

"...the greatest thing we can do is to let somebody know that they're loved and capable of loving."

Loved, and capable of loving.

Given the chance to see a wrong, and right it. Being seen for the good in their hearts. Being thanked in return, for caring.

That's been my personal quest as a fundraising copywriter from the start.

To help donors feel "seen" for their generosity... for their commitment... for their loyalty... to rally them to keep fighting the good fight. To help when they can.

Of his famous theme song that started each new episode, Fred Rogers said in the documentary that he saw "Won't you be my neighbor?" as an invitation.

<u>An invitation for somebody to be close to you</u>.

Today, I invite you.

To be my neighbor in gratitude. To help your donors feel seen. To keep them close to you, and to your beneficiaries, and to your hardworking staff.

Close to the urgent work they support.

In our final moments together, I want to share with you how much that will mean to your donors when you help them know they are seen and appreciated.

I know, because it happens every time thanking gets better.

Donors begin to send, phone in, and email their own thanks in return.

In fact, sprinkled throughout this book you've already seen excerpted quotes from real-life examples of what I've come to call "supporter fan mail."

I think of them as donor love letters to humanity and a better world.

Because, as you'll see illustrated below, the letters and cards donors send are far more beautiful than the name "fan mail" implies.

The original letters were handwritten, and Designer Sandie has captured that feel for me here, grammatical eccentricities and all, to protect donor privacy:

I am very impressed with your beautiful letter saying thank you for my donation. It might as well have been 1,000 dollars! But I came to realize when reading it how important every donation is.

Your explanation of how the money is spent was so honest and believable.

My husband and I have booked a tour on [date] and we are both looking forward to the visit. The work you and your team do is amazing and we are glad to give some assistance to your cause...God Bless your excellent work.

Lots of Love + Best Wishes,
A.M. and W.B.

And the second:

Through your correspondence and my visit last year I have gotten to know you the wonderful staff who "are there" for all who need a welcoming heart and listening ear. All of this is a very touching and enriching experience for me.

This donor signed this letter, *"Yours sincerely and gratefully."*
She had donated... and yet... <u>she</u> **was the one who was grateful!**

This is what it's about, people: the beating heart of this book.

The beating heart of fundraising, and donor communications, too.

You can't see me at the moment I wrote this, or know my feelings. But I am right now picturing the future you.

The thankologist. The world-changer.

Reading through the first of the heartfelt letters you receive back from donors. Dedicated to your supporters. Ready to do even more.

I'm beyond grateful for your tenacity. Your resolve to get this right.

Donors may never know how fortunate they are to have you on their side.

But if I had a crystal ball, I'm willing to bet that in the years to come, they'll return your hard work in enthusiasm, gratitude, loyalty, and yes, generosity.

That's how wonderful your donors are.

Thank you, thankologist, for being you. Thank you so much for reading.

Now go forth with great heart and give your donors something beautiful.

Believe me, they will love you for it. And humanity will be better for it, too.

APPENDICES:

A thankologist's toolbox of user-ready tips and tidbits

"Silent gratitude isn't very much use to anyone."

— **Gertrude Stein,** *American writer*

APPENDIX

I

Because Lisa loves you and wants you to thank well:
Pre-written leads, postscripts, and more

As someone who earns her keep as a copywriter, no one can relate more intimately than I can to the dread fear created by the blank page.

I never want that fear to keep you from your next great donor thank-you.

That's why, in this part of the book, you'll find free phrases you can swipe that are all my own. And they are my gift to you. Call on them like trusty friends, whenever you need a bit of inspiration, or the blank page leaves you cold.

Then get busy writing.

11 adaptable thank-you leads that beat *On behalf of*:

Leads that are directly relevant to the specific organization, appeal, or newsletter that prompted the donor to give are always preferred.

By relevant, I mean something like, *"When the last chain falls to the ground... when their captors are put to justice... when antitethering is forever the law of the land... the animals will have you to thank for it."*

Or, *"If not for you, Fintan's story might have waned like a whisper. Just one more homeless man lost to the streets."*

<u>But sometimes you can't be directly relevant.</u>

In these cases, the following all-purpose leads are handy, and might inspire your thinking about other 1-2 line leads of your own:

- ♥ You, wonderful you.

- ♥ What a remarkable thing you have done.

- ♥ We needed you, and you were there.

- ♥ How did you come to be so kind and generous? Thank you.

- ♥ One in a million. That's what you are.

- ♥ Somewhere in the darkness, a [hungry child/homeless animal/etc.] cried out for help. And because of your generosity, a caring voice was there to answer.

- ♥ Today the future shines a little brighter, because you chose to give.

- ♥ It's been said that gratitude is the language of the heart, and I believe it's true. I believe, because of you.

- ♥ Generosity. Compassion. Truth. Justice. Today I know you stand for all of these things, and I know because you chose to make a generous donation to [XXX charity].

- ♥ Just when it seemed all hope was lost, you came along and saved the day. [Thank you for being the heart of XYZ charity.]

- ♥ Close your eyes... can you feel it? Listen closely... can you hear it? Brave new beginnings are unfolding every day here, thanks to you.

Moving on to thank-you letter sign-offs that say more than "Sincerely,":

Way back in the earliest chapters of this book, we talked about who should sign your letter and some of the ways you might craft a more inspiring sign-off for your thank-yous… something that says a bit more than "Sincerely."

Use these sign-offs just as they are, or to inspire your own captivating closing:

- ♥ Until every companion animal has a home,
- ♥ With deepest gratitude from all of us here,
- ♥ We'd be lost without you,
- ♥ Here's to every new tomorrow,
- ♥ Thank you for being their true companion,
- ♥ Thank you for caring so much about [this work of the heart/homeless animals/the future of education/etc.],
- ♥ Thank you for extending a lifeline to [animals/people in need etc.],
- ♥ Thank you for lighting the spark for [tomorrow's medical breakthroughs, etc.]
- ♥ With all my thanks,
- ♥ From our hearts to yours,
- ♥ Thank you for victories big and small,
- ♥ You are always in our hearts,

And here are a handful of pre-written postscripts to test, try, and tweak:

What I hope you'll see here is how flexible the postscript is. Whether it's the contact info, or to note an enclosure or something that's forthcoming, or an invitation – even the tax disclaimer if you need one – you can mix, match, and modify once you get the hang of it.

1. **The short and sweet P.S.:**

P.S. If you have questions about your gift, the work, or the animals, <u>please</u> call us at [phone number] or email [supportercare@xyz.org]. We are here and always happy to help you. All my thanks again.

2. **The invitation to an event P.S.:**

> P.S. In case you missed it in your [donor newsletter], I want to personally invite you to [name of event] on [day/date/time]. It's [event details such as: held each year in honor of your incredible support, and admission is free.] You are very welcome to bring your friends and family, we'd love to see you there. For details ring [staff name] at [phone]. Again, all my gratitude for all you do.

3. **The IRS tax disclaimer P.S. (we do lots of experimenting with the position of the disclaimer – and again, clear with your legal team first):**

> P.S. Remember to keep this letter as your tax receipt for [YEAR], to conserve resources. It lets you know [charity name] is a registered 501(c)(3) organization and that no goods or services were provided in exchange for your very kind, tax-deductible donation. If you have any questions about your gift, or the work, <u>please</u> call or email. We are so grateful you're with us. Thank you again.

4. **The how you can reach us P.S.:**

> P.S. If you ever have questions, or you'd like to learn more about becoming [a volunteer/one of our citizen scientists], please visit us online at [URL], follow the good work you support on Facebook, or call us directly at [charity phone number]. And thank you again.

5. **The when you'll next hear from us (when your nonprofit doesn't yet have a newsletter) P.S.:**

> P.S. I promise to keep you updated via Facebook (where you'll find all the news and lots of photos of the work you make possible), on the [Name of Nonprofit] website at [URL], and as I often can, by email and mail. And if you ever have questions, please call us at [phone] – we'd love to hear from you. Again, thank you. You are a true friend to [animals/children/etc.]!

6. **The let's test a friendly legacy mention (providing you have a bequest guide that isn't institutional and off-putting) P.S:**

> P.S. Have you always wanted to be remembered as a true friend to [beneficiaries]? I hope you'll consider including a bequest of any size to [Name of Nonprofit] in your Will, and do good for [beneficiaries] in need even after you're gone. We have an [estate planning guide] that many of our supporters find really helpful, and you can find it here, for free: **[URL]**. If you've any questions, give [legacy officer] a call at [direct line]. Thank you so much.
>
> *Note: You can (and should) have legacy details on your website, including sample language donors can use to include you in their will. Even if you don't have a bequest guide, you can modify the language to let people know they can learn more and find sample language online.*

7. **The we met the match! P.S.:**

> P.S. I'm so pleased to let you know that your donation has been [doubled] at no extra cost to you in our [$ total amount of matching challenge] matching challenge, [doubling] the good you do! Please call us anytime at [phone number] if you have questions or if you'd ever like to visit us. It will be our great joy to welcome you. All my thanks to you, again – we wouldn't be here without you.

8. **The first gift and a welcome pack's coming P.S.:**

> P.S. Our next supporter newsletter, [name of newsletter], will reach you in [month]. Meanwhile watch for your heartfelt welcome pack arriving shortly, where I share some of the stories of lives that you're changing. I hope you enjoy it! And if for any reason you ever need to reach us, just call: we're here for you at [phone number]. Thank you again!

APPENDIX

II

Roger Craver's foolproof formula for calculating your nonprofit's donor retention rate

In Roger Craver's *Retention Fundraising* there is an exceptional example of the importance of donor retention that showed, specifically, the cumulative effect of a ten-percentage point difference in retention over fourteen years – at a charity with 5,000 donors, on an average gift of $200.

Over those 14 years, donors with a 51% retention rate gave... wait for it... more than $450,000 more than donors with a 41% retention rate.

<u>Nearly half a million dollars</u>.

He goes on to say:

"Few fundraising investments produce a greater return than those made for the purpose of increasing retention rates."

Knowing that, you'd be astonished at the number of nonprofits I speak with that <u>still</u> don't calculate and track their donor retention rates.

I never want that to happen to you. Neither does Roger Craver.

Roger generously agreed to let me feature his retention rate formula here, so you'll always know where you stand: [55]

Step 1: Count the total number of donors who gave in your most recent calendar or fiscal year.

Step 2: Divide the number of donors who made a donation in year 2 by the total in Step 1.

Step 3: Multiply the result from Step 2 by 100 to obtain your retention rate as a percentage.

And... from the wise and generous fundraisers at Bloomerang, as shared in Craver's book, witness the jaw-dropping change in total return on a 10% difference in donor retention (just one extra donor in ten), over just 14 years:

Original Retention Rate: 41%				Improved Retention Rate: 51%			
Year	Donors	Avg. Gift*	Total	Year	Donors	Avg. Gift*	Total
Start	5,000	$ 200.00		Start	5,000	$ 200.00	
2	2,050	$ 220.00	$ 451,000	2	2,550	$ 220.00	$ 561,000
3	841	$ 242.00	$ 203,401	3	1,301	$ 242.00	$ 314,721
4	345	$ 266.20	$ 91,734	4	663	$ 266.20	$ 176,558
5	141	$ 292.82	$ 41,372	5	338	$ 292.82	$ 99,049
6	58	$ 322.10	$ 18,659	6	173	$ 322.10	$ 55,567
7	24	$ 354.31	$ 8,415	7	88	$ 354.31	$ 31,173
8	10	$ 389.74	$ 3,795	8	45	$ 389.74	$ 17,488
9	4	$ 428.72	$ 1,712	9	23	$ 428.72	$ 9,811
10	2	$ 471.59	$ 772	10	12	$ 471.59	$ 5,504
11	—	—	—	11	6	$ 518.75	$ 3,088
12	—	—	—	12	3	$ 570.62	$ 1,732
13	—	—	—	13	2	$ 627.69	$ 972
14	—	—	—	14	1	$ 690.45	$ 545

Grand Total from Original Donors: **$ 820,859**   Grand Total from Original Donors: **$ 1,277,208**

Total Savings: $ 456,349

Source: "A Guide to Donor Retention," Bloomerang. Free online at: https://bloomerang.co/blog/donor-retention/.

---

55 Roger Craver, *Retention Fundraising*, September 2014, page 127. https://hilborn-civilsectorpress.com/products/retention-fundraising

APPENDIX

III

The better donation thank-you letter checklist ☑

From Lisa Sargent's Free Thank-You Letter Clinics on SOFII, www.sofii.org
(For a free, printable PDF, visit lisasargent.com/resources)

- ☐ Is it personalized? (As in "Dear Lisa" vs. "Dear Friend")
- ☐ Is the gift amount noted?
  Note: Some fundraisers say that you need to send a thank-you *without* the gift amount, and separately, later, an official receipt. Over 10+ years of including the gift amount in a single thank-you letter, and eliminating a separate receipt, we've found that it is well-received, shows wise and careful stewardship, delivers good retention, and saves money.
- ☐ Do you start with something other than "Thank you for your gift of..."?
- ☐ Are you using an exciting lead?
- ☐ Do you tell the donor when and how they will next hear from you?
- ☐ If this is a repeat gift, do you also thank donor for their:
  - ○ Past generosity (and indicate all it's made possible), and
  - ○ Continued contributions/support
- ☐ If this is a gift membership (meaning made by someone else on giftee's behalf):
  - ○ Do not thank the giftee, but talk about what "this kind gift makes possible"
  - ○ Send a thank you letter to the giftor so they know their gift has been made as intended and that giftee will be notified
- ☐ Say something new or timely in the P.S. – videos online, a holiday message, an upcoming opportunity to visit or meet with you, etc.
- ☐ Include a contact number donor can use if they have questions (you can add an e-mail, but <u>not</u> the generic "info@yourorg.org." Direct them to a living, breathing human, please.)

- ☐ Do you need to thank them for something specific? For example:
  - ○ Membership renewal
  - ○ Holiday appeal
  - ○ Memorial/tribute donation
  - ○ Capital campaign (focus on all the good this new building/machine/ wing will do)
- ☐ Do you need to reference something specific? For example:
  - ○ A gift you'll be sending
  - ○ A welcome pack arriving
  - ○ A certificate or photo you've enclosed
- ☐ Do you have a website? Mention it in the letter, with a simple call-to-action to drive them there. ("Keep up with all the ways you're helping XYZ at www.XYZ.org.")
- ☐ And remember to:
  - ○ Keep the letter short (3-4 paras plus a P.S.)
  - ○ Add required tax-deductible language
- ☐ Share with them "all your gift makes possible..."
- ☐ Use more "you" than "we" and "our."
- ☐ Say thank you more than once.
- ☐ Use the right signatory/signer
  - ○ Almost always, President, Executive Director, or CEO: thank-yous should come from the top
- ☐ Proof your letter:
  - ○ Use spell check
  - ○ Print the letter and read it out loud, word for word
- ☐ If you can, hand-sign them all. If you have too many donors, determine an amount at which you or a board member will hand-sign. And an amount for a phone call.
- ☐ In my world, the vast majority of donation thank-you letters do not include:
  - ○ An additional "hard ask" for a donation (sometimes, we mention legacy/gifts-in-wills)
  - ○ An upgrade to monthly giving or other program
  - ○ Yours to test/track: a reply envelope. Although my thank-you letters almost never include a direct ask to give again, many of my clients do include a postage-paid/Freepost reply envelope. Over both the short and long hauls, it hasn't seemed to affect retention either way.

APPENDIX

IV

50 qualities you can recognize in your donors to deepen connection:
My original 13, plus 37 more for you to use

Over my morning cup of coffee on February 16, 2019 I posted a tiny, two minute tweet over on my @lisasargent2 Twitter (now X) thread that sped around the world in ways I never could have imagined. It appears that LOTS of nonprofit folks were interested in doing a better job of thanking their donors — and that tweet has since been used in loads of presentations, including some of my own [56]. So, just for you here, I'm including my 2019 tweet and my list of the 13 originals below, and adding 37 more...

Lisa's original 13 qualities you can recognize in your donors to deepen connection: Thank you for your...

- ♥ courage
- ♥ faith
- ♥ trust
- ♥ concern
- ♥ loyalty
- ♥ dedication
- ♥ sense of justice

---

56 One of those is the mini-webinar, "How to Write Your Best-Ever Donation Thank-You Letter... Every Time!" by yours truly, for my brilliant friends at Moceanic. [online, through Moceanic's for-purchase, and well-worth-it annual membership] https://www.moceanic.com/.

- vision
- resolve
- integrity
- kindness
- steadfastness
- understanding
- compassion

Plus – *directly from my keyboard to yours* **– 37 more you can use: Thank you for...**

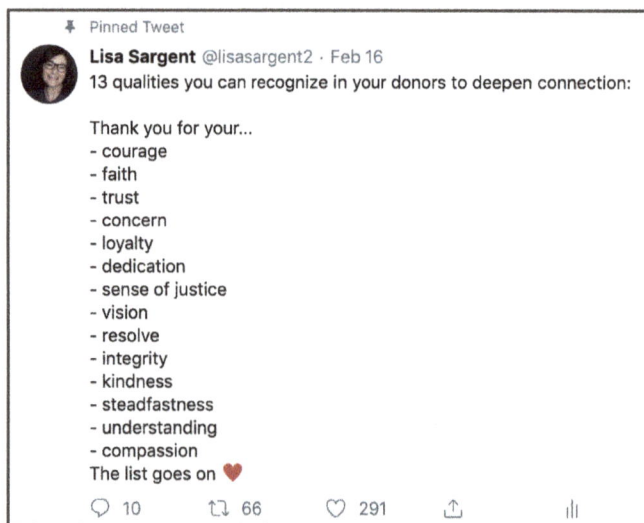

📌 Pinned Tweet

Lisa Sargent @lisasargent2 · Feb 16
13 qualities you can recognize in your donors to deepen connection:

Thank you for your...
- courage
- faith
- trust
- concern
- loyalty
- dedication
- sense of justice
- vision
- resolve
- integrity
- kindness
- steadfastness
- understanding
- compassion
The list goes on ❤️

💬 10   🔁 66   ♡ 291   ⬆️   📊

- your grace and generosity
- your fighting spirit
- your heart for (animals, world change, etc.)
- your commitment to (ending oppression, etc.)
- believing in a better tomorrow
- opening a door to tomorrow
- never turning away
- staying by our side
- walking beside (beneficiaries)
- being precisely who you are
- being you
- being there
- caring as much as you do
- taking the time to give
- taking the time to care

- ❤ holding fast to what's right
- ❤ the gift that you are
- ❤ hope and healing
- ❤ hope where there was none before
- ❤ every new future
- ❤ every new beginning
- ❤ every new breakthrough
- ❤ every first step
- ❤ growth and change
- ❤ each new chance
- ❤ each life you touch
- ❤ the promise of tomorrow
- ❤ the relief and goodness you bring
- ❤ victories little and large
- ❤ the sparkle in every smile
- ❤ keeping our lights on and our doors open
- ❤ keeping staff in the field
- ❤ believing that true change is possible
- ❤ staying through thick and thin
- ❤ your commitment to a brighter future
- ❤ being a force for good
- ❤ changing the world.

Lisa Sargent
@lisasargent2

Recognizing donor identities, cont'd. Some basic phrases I'm experimenting with based on recent research by @AdrianSargeant and others:

1. Thank you for being a person who...
2. Because you are someone who...
3. As a supporter to XYZcharity, you have shown you are someone who...

9:54 AM · Feb 16, 2019 · Twitter for iPhone

⏐⏐ View Tweet activity

14 Retweets   **90** Likes

And thank you too, thankologist, for changing the world. Today, tomorrow, and always. Write with love... go forth with great heart... and may your words, from now until forever, work for good. – Lisa xx

About the Author

LISA SARGENT is an award-winning fundraising copywriter, nonprofit educator, and story strategist on a mission to transform the way nonprofits communicate with their donors. Sargent is a contributing author to the acclaimed decision science book *Change for Better*, and her free Donor Thank-You Clinics were named one of the world's "top 10 gifts for fundraisers" by SOFII (Showcase of Fundraising Innovation and Inspiration). Sargent is co-author of *Lessons from Merchants Quay Ireland*, a widely acclaimed case history on the remarkable outcome of proper donor care, created at the invitation of the Commission on the Donor Experience. With a Certificate in Philanthropic Psychology with Distinction from the Institute for Sustainable Philanthropy, Sargent writes, speaks, and trains on what works: proven production perspectives, results-based copywriting and creative tips, actionable strategies, and a bounty of behavioral science delivered with a perennial passion for building a better world. She wears her heart on her sleeve for clients past and present including: Trócaire, Best Friends Animal Society, Merchants Quay Ireland, ChildVision, St. Helena Hospital Foundation, Barretstown, Shriners Hospitals for Children, Animals Asia, and Northwestern Memorial Foundation, among others. Sargent lives in New Hampshire with her husband and giant rescued Great Pyrenees and is the adoring mom of a tool-and-die-maker daughter, who clearly got all her math skills from her father.

Subscribe to Lisa's free newsletter, The Loyalty Letter, at **lisasargent.com**, and follow Lisa on LinkedIn at **linkedin.com/in/lisasargent**.